Janet,

Celebrate
Jesus!

Lori Salierno

Rom 12:11

DESIGNED FOR

EXCELLENCE

BY LORI SALIERNO
WITH ESTHER BAILEY

Church Ministries Division
Warner Press
Anderson, Indiana

All Scripture quotations, unless otherwise noted, are from the New Revised Standard Version of the Bible, copyright ©1989 by the Division of Christian Education of the National Council of the Churches of Christ in the USA, or the HOLY BIBLE, NEW INTERNATIONAL VERSION®. Copyright © 1973, 1978,1984 International Bible Society. Used by permission of Zondervan Bible Publishers. All rights reserved.

© 1995 by Warner Press
ISBN #0-87162-681-0   Stock #D3575
UPC # 730817 220611

Second Edition
© 1996 by Church Ministries Division, Warner Press

Warner Press, Anderson, Indiana
David C. Shultz, Editor in Chief
Dan Harman, Book Editor
C. D. Oliver, Jr, Editor
Paul Johnson, Cover design

Contents

Part I: Seeking Personal Excellence

Part II: Excellence in Relationships

Part III: Serving with Excellence

Foreword

I regard everything as loss because of the surpassing value of knowing Christ Jesus my Lord. For his sake I have suffered the loss of all things, and regard them as rubbish, in order that I may gain Christ.

—Philippians 3:8

Lori Salierno is an intriguing, captivating, winsome witness for Jesus Christ. Boundless energy and sometimes audacious courage have brought to this wonderful storyteller a wealth of experiences worth sharing. Everyone should be fortunate enough to know Lori. *Designed for Excellence* provides a fresh, readable opportunity to sit alongside this remarkable person and to look through the window of her experiences into the faith claims of Christ—which can touch one's life and change one's living.

Designed for Excellence leaps out of a commitment to the truth of Philippians 3:8 to launch a personal testimony challenging readers to evaluate their spiritual status. Lori insists on encounters, demands responses, wants to change the world, and is in a hurry to get the job done now. All this makes for exciting reading and for more important conversations within the heart of the reader about the things that truly matter in a world claiming our allegiances. Lori encourages the reader to move from a mere profession of faith to a life-changing encounter with Jesus the Christ.

The chapters in this book deal with real-life problems that confront us all but especially today's youth. Young people learn it is all right to be Christians. They learn they can have fun, achieve their goals, and build fulfilling relationships while serving God.

Lori addresses issues that usually generate confusion and conflict such as sexuality and peer pressure; yet she explores them in sufficient depth to offer sound, biblical advice. She explains why God calls for a lifestyle above the level of mediocrity. She provides practical steps to show her readers how to attain excellence in their lives through God's design. Prayer and Bible reading are projected as important habits for knowing God. Thus, a daily devotional life becomes a privilege rather than a duty.

Designed for Excellence offers an attractive high road for those who want to travel in life all the way to joy. Whether discerning God's call, learning how to pray, or living out personal convictions, the true stories, observations, and illustrations from Lori's life will illustrate how God uses ordinary people to accomplish extraordinary results. Lori invites young people and old alike to the exuberance of a faith-filled party where the celebration is to be in the presence of the Lord and in following the Lord's ways. She lifts the reader's vision to the kind of excellence that makes one proud to look in the mirror and be named among the children of God. She confronts lesser choices with judgment. She names the weaknesses of a mediocre life. In the end, she makes best friends of her readers and motivates those along the journey to want to experience the best that God has to offer. *Designed for Excellence* is Lori Salierno's gift to the thousands who hear her speak each year and would love to have an extended conversation with her. In enduring ways, she shares the best of her thinking. This is a book that will change lives.

Enjoy the journey. With Lori Salierno behind the wheel, the ride will be unforgettable.

—James L. Edwards
President, Anderson University

These pages are dedicated
to the memory of Marie Strong—
professor, mentor, and friend.
It was her constant encouragement
that caused me even to attempt this book.

Part I
Seeking Personal Excellence

Chapter 1

The Party's on God

I travel often by airplane. Since I'm always looking for an opportunity to share the gospel, I pray for the people who will sit next to me on the plane. I sometimes try to sit in the middle seat so, in case the person on my right doesn't want to talk, I can talk to the person on my left and tell him or her what Jesus Christ has done for me.

One morning the plane wasn't crowded so I sat by the window. As I prayed for the one who would sit next to me, a sharp-looking businessman took the aisle seat. He was polished from head to toe. When the plane reached cruising altitude, he opened his personal computer and started typing.

I tried to get an idea of what he was doing, but he paid me no attention. Finally I said, "Hi, sir. My name is Lori. What's yours?"

He kept typing.

I thought his ears might be clogged up due to the altitude, so I turned up the volume on my voice. I said, "Hello. My name is Lori. What's yours?"

Without looking up he said, "I heard you the first time. But, lady, I have no time to talk to you right now."

Not willing to give up, I prodded, "So, like, are you a major, important person or something?" He kept typing. I got the message that he didn't want to talk, so I started sending "prayer arrows" at him because I wanted him to know about the Lord.

Finally he said, "Okay, I want you to know I am important."

"You are?" I hoped the enthusiastic ring in my voice would invite further conversation.

"Yes," he said. "When I came into this company sales were down, morale was down, and the company was about to go under. Since they hired me sales are up, morale is up, and we're successful. All that can be attributed to me, and I want you to know I am important."

"Wow! You have a healthy self-image too," I said.

"Well, you must have a healthy self-image in my line of work. I feel good about what I've done." He paused for a moment and then perhaps out of polite obligation said, "So, what do you do for a living?"

I could have told him I am a minister and ended the conversation right there. Instead, I chose to whet his curiosity with, "I party."

"I didn't ask you what you do on weekends. What do you do during the week?"

Trying to project the joy that bubbled inside me, I said, "I told you. I party."

His mouth flew open and he said, "You party Monday through Sunday?"

"That's right."

He frowned. "What does your boss say about that?"

"My boss throws the parties," I said, confident that I spoke the truth.

"You mean your boss parties with you?"

"You got it!"

I could almost see the wheels spinning in his head. "Is your boss wealthy or something?" he ventured.

"My boss is the wealthiest person ever and all he has is mine, just for the asking!"

The man closed his computer and asked, "Well, is he famous?"

An aura of mystery mounted. I loved it. "He is so famous that if I spoke his first name everyone would know who he is."

His gaze intensified as he searched my eyes. "Lady, who are you?"

"Pretty important, huh?"

"What I want to know is, can I cash in on the deal?"

"Just like that," I said as I snapped my fingers.

"But your boss doesn't even know me."

"You'd be surprised what my boss knows about you." With intrigue building to the max, I wondered where our conversation would lead us.

"Well," he said somewhat impatiently, "what's his name?"

The dramatic moment had come, but I did not know how this young tycoon might handle my answer. "I'm not sure I should reveal his name," I said.

"Lady, you just threw me a line and I grabbed it," he said. "Either admit you're a big fake or tell me his name."

"Lean over the seat," I said. As he leaned toward me I leaned toward him. Looking him straight in the eyes and with deep conviction, I said, "My boss's name is Jesus Christ."

His reaction resembled that of a child who had for the first time watched a balloon inflate only to see it pricked with a pin. He thought me to be odd, but I believe my message got through to him. I believe he will remember for a long time the day when the Christian life was portrayed to him as a life of celebration.

Many people believe that the Christian life is dull. Some Christians even believe they are missing out on the fun because they serve the Lord. That idea comes from Satan. God doesn't want us to miss out on anything good in life. God's salvation offers us a joyful life.

A Joyful Theme

The Bible records some 483 references to joy. Pretty impressive, huh? That doesn't include references to words such as *delight* or *gladness*.

For example, the theme of joy abounds throughout the Psalms. "The precepts of the LORD are right, rejoicing the heart" (19:8). "Make a joyful noise to the LORD, all the earth" (100:1). Indeed, Christians do have something to shout about.

The prophet Isaiah also left a legacy of joy in his writings. "O dwellers in the dust, awake and sing for joy!" (26:19). "I will greatly rejoice in the LORD, / my whole being shall exult in my God; / for he has clothed me with the garments of salvation, / he has covered me with the robe of righteousness" (61:10). The emphasis on salvation and righteousness accents the reason for our joy.

When Jesus was born, God threw the grandest party of all time. What host or hostess could match the appearance of an angelic chorus singing about good news of great joy? (Luke 2:10). The reason for the party was the fulfillment of the promise of forgiveness. We who have been set free from sin's bondage through the blood of Jesus have just begun to live life to the fullest.

Joyful Celebration Glorifies God

Would you like to throw a birthday party for a friend who sat in the corner looking glum while everyone else had a great time? If the angels in heaven rejoiced at our new birth, doesn't God want us to celebrate as well?

Our joy pleases God. Do you realize Christians are a sweet-smelling fragrance to God? Our lives become "the aroma of Christ to God among those who are being saved and among those who are perishing" (2 Corinthians 2:15). Our joy inspires other believers (those who are being saved) and is attractive to the unchurched (those who are perishing). As we joyfully celebrate our victory in Jesus, we encourage other Christians who may be going through a difficult time. Simply by revealing the joy of the Lord, we cause the ungodly to recognize there is value in serving God.

Armed with good reasons to be people of joy, we might ask, How can we participate in the party God gives every day of the week? Can anyone get in on the celebration, regardless of personality traits or circumstances?

When I received an invitation to go to Africa to address missionaries from five countries, I was thrilled. This is a great opportunity, I thought.

Just before I was to speak, the host told me the missionaries desperately needed inspiration and encouragement because they were physically worn out.

As everyone arrived, I felt myself getting nervous. These people had served the Lord faithfully for many years. Their lives represented the kind of sacrifice I had not made. They looked tired. What might I say to inspire and encourage them? I prayed, "Lord, let me inspire them through you."

As I began to speak I said, "I don't know much about Africa. I don't understand the problems you face. Although I can't offer you wise advice, I'd like to remind you of the joy of the Lord." At that point the Holy Spirit seemed to flood my soul with an extra measure of joy. The missionaries quickly captured that joy and we became kindred spirits—laughing, weeping, and praying together. We had a party that could not be equaled this side of heaven.

Joy is an attitude rather than a feeling. Whether we have a personality that bubbles over or bombs out, we can choose to base our attitudes on the victory we share in Christ. We can develop an attitude of joy by practicing the following disciplines.

1. Acknowledge God's Presence

Trying to comprehend the nature of God just about blows me away. God is majestic, yet chooses to be enriched by the praises of faithful people. Isn't that amazing? A mighty God desires communion with you and me! The thought is awesome!

Do you realize that praise is the one thing we do for God that God cannot do alone? What an incredible thought! Praise is the one gift we can give to the one who has given so much to us. Communion with God is a privilege. "Tremble, O earth, at the presence of the LORD" (Psalm 114:7), but "[God makes us] glad with the joy of [divine] presence" (21:6).

You can practice being aware of God's presence no matter where you are or what you are doing. Wake up in the morning and say, "God, I'm going to give you a standing ovation today." During a lecture, or while taking a test, take three seconds and say, "Lord, I know you're here and I love you." Allow gratitude to flow from your heart as well as from your lips as you offer a prayer before meals. Acknowledge God's presence on the tennis court, on a date, or while watching television. Develop the habit of talking and listening to God about all of your activities.

At first you may feel like a phony praising God a hundred times a day, but do it anyway. Before long God's presence will become real and your worship will become a natural part of life.

2. Program Your Mind with Joy

Life does not always cooperate with our intentions to party with the Lord. After twenty-five years in ministry, the Apostle Paul had established churches, trained ministers, and worked miracles in the name of Jesus. Later in his life, chained to prison guards, Paul could have been discouraged and refused to nurture the joy of his salvation. He didn't. He continued to preach the good news and to write letters to different congregations he had helped establish.

From his jail cell, Paul wrote, "Rejoice in the Lord always" (Philippians 4:4). Now, if I had been in jail, I would have had trouble writing about joy. Paul repeated the advice. "Again I will say, Rejoice." He made the joy of the Lord the theme of his letter to the Philippians. In verse eight of that chapter, Paul suggested appropriate topics for Christians to think about—truth, justice, and purity are a few. "If there is any excellence and if there is anything worthy of praise," Paul wrote, "think about these things."

It takes discipline to program your mind with joy. A teacher may grade your paper unfairly. Someone may spread a vicious rumor about you. A friendship may turn sour. You may not be able to get a job, or you may not have the money to go to college. Paul wrote, "In any and all circumstances I have learned the secret of being well-fed and of going hungry, of having plenty and of being in need" (Philippians 4:12). You may hurt inside, but you can still have the kind of joy that's anchored in God's love.

God's joy is like a rock. I suggest a practical way to help you program your mind with that joy. Find a small, well-rounded rock. With a felt tip pen, print the word *joy* on top of the rock. Keep it on your desk or near your bed. When life shoots harmful arrows your way to knock you down, deflect those arrows toward the rock. Then imagine them breaking into little pieces as soon as they hit the rock of your salvation. Claim victory as you say in your heart, "I will never allow anyone or any circumstance to rob me of my joy in the Lord."

3. Create a Momentous Occasion

Have you ever noticed that life sometimes gets monotonous? You go to the same classes with the same teachers and receive the same kinds of assignments. You live in the same place and eat the same kinds of food day after day.

My husband, Kurt, and I tend to get in a rut occasionally. We get up in the morning, eat breakfast, go to church, make calls, go home, eat supper, go back to church, go home, and go to bed. Day in and day out, the routine sometimes becomes too methodical for my free spirit.

One Friday, Kurt decided to take the youth group on an overnight camp-out. I decided I was going to break out of my rut or else. As soon as I drove down the street and saw a sign that read *Rent a Vette*, I got a clue about how I would get out of my rut.

On Saturday when Kurt returned the youth group to the church, I drove onto the parking lot in the Corvette. As I circled the parking lot, I raced the engine and everyone looked up except my task-oriented, type *A* personality husband. He had his head down and was helping the kids sort out their gear. One of the guys named Chris said, "Check out the chick in the Corvette!" Kurt kept working. I made another circle around the parking lot and then stopped directly in front of Kurt. He continued working, but Chris said, "Hey, Kurt, the chick in the Corvette is your wife."

That got his attention! Kurt looked up and said, "What are you doing?"

"Hi, sweetheart," I said. "I thought I'd buy you a Corvette to get you out of your rut."

"I gotta get me a woman like that!" Chris said.

Kurt wasn't quite as enthusiastic. "You didn't buy that," he said.

"Yes I did, Kurt."

"Lori, what did you do?"

I said, "Kurt, I did a tremendous thing for you. I rented this convertible for you for twenty-four hours."

"In that case, move over," he said. "I want behind the wheel."

Occasionally we need to spice up our lives with a momentous event. Mary sponsored a gala affair when she broke the perfume jar and spilled the contents over the feet of Jesus. The fragrance of her celebration filled the entire room (John 12:3).

You can't literally anoint the feet of Jesus. Maybe you can't rent a Corvette, but you can find a way to create a momentous occasion in your life. Make a new friend or look up a childhood playmate. Write your parents a letter of appreciation without even hinting for money. Their reaction will generate major excitement. If you're the studious type, go for an outdoor adventure. If you're the venturesome type, write a poem or a prayer. Any activity that differs from the everyday norm will break up your boredom and perk up your spirits.

4. Savor Joy in the Ordinary

Although we can temporarily escape a humdrum existence, most of life must be lived in the commonplace. To be responsible people we must work hard, study hard, and plan for the future. That means taking time out from the party to tend to the necessary details of life.

While we can't be in a party mood all the time, we can still be persons of joy regardless of what we're doing. Did you know that God has little pockets of joy hidden among the ordinary events in a day's schedule?

An alarm wakes you in the morning. You didn't get enough sleep. You would rather turn over and forget responsibility, but you struggle to your feet. A scripture comes to your mind. "This is the day that the LORD has made; / let us rejoice and be glad in it" (Psalm 118:24). You have just popped open one of God's pockets of delight and you are better prepared to face the day. You look outside. It is raining. Rain usually depresses you, but you remember the glorious sunset from the previous evening. Another pocket of delight pops up in your mind.

You go to school or work. The conversation centers on the news of the day. Someone you know was picked up for shoplifting. You're sorry that someone else is in trouble. At the same time, though, your mind finds another one of God's pockets of delight. You realize you could have been the offender had it not been for the protective power of the Holy Spirit.

As pressures build during the day, you have no time to yourself. You can merely acknowledge a compliment and return the smile of a stranger, but you learn to savor those pockets of joy in everyday life.

When you get home, you find a card from your favorite aunt. You laugh at her sense of humor and read between the lines to detect her love for you. Your parents are engrossed in their own affairs, but evidence of love and affection carries through from former conversations.

While preparing for bed, you realize it has been a good day. Many things went wrong and nothing sensational happened. It was an ordinary day, but little pockets of delight added up to provide a cause for a big celebration.

With God's party in full swing, are you ready to participate? Will you lift your heart in praise to God who sent Jesus to bring abundant life to us? Will you recognize that life can beat you up but it can't beat you down if the joy of the Lord is your strength? If life has grown stale for you, God is ready to restore your joy. You can then join the royal party prepared for you by the King of kings.

***

Read Philemon 1–7, and focus on verse 7. Name several persons who are sources of joy to you.

_____

_____

_____

_____

In your own words write what someone has done in the past week to bring you joy.

_____

_____

_____

_____

Write what you will you do this week to add to another person's joy.

_____

_____

_____

_____

Pray the following prayer.

God, thank you for calling me to be a joyful person, a person of celebration. Thank you for the gift of life through your Son, Jesus Christ. I want to take hold of life and kiss it smack-dab in the face because of the victory that is mine through Jesus.

Help me to become more aware of your presence. Help me identify the pockets of joy you have prepared for me. Help me to maintain my joy through times of ecstasy and times of sorrow. I can do these things because you are my strength. You are my portion. You are my Lord. In Jesus' name I pray. Amen.

Chapter 2
Front-Burner Religion

I remember the day that Jesus came into my life. It was a real and definite experience.

I was reared in a pastor's home. Everything our family did revolved around church. My parents read me Bible stories. I learned to pray at mealtimes and at bedtime; I learned to believe God would hear and answer my prayers. Not only did my parents teach me to be a Christian, they practiced everything they taught. It would have been easy for me to feel satisfied with my "inherited" religious experience.

When I was nine years old, my parents took me to an old-time camp meeting in Polluck, Louisiana. A large tent served as the church building and the ground allowed my friends and me to entertain ourselves by scratching in the dirt floor.

"Look what I found," one of my friends whispered during a service one night as she held up a dime she found in the dirt. From then on we spent much of our time looking for coins.

One evening I was busy doodling in the dirt when I heard the evangelist say, "Do you know Jesus Christ as your personal Savior?" I had heard my father ask the same question many times, but this time something pierced my heart. I looked up to give the preacher my full attention and heard him ask other questions. "Have you invited Jesus Christ into your heart? Does he reign in your life as Lord?" I could not continue playing with my friends because the preacher's questions overwhelmed me. For the first time in my life the weight of my sin consumed me.

After the service I had started toward my mother when I tripped over an exposed root of a tree. Instantly I burst into tears that mounted into uncontrollable sobs.

"Why is Lori crying so hard?" a woman asked my mother. "She really didn't get hurt that badly."

My mother gathered me into her arms and comforted me. I distinctly remember her words to her friend. "Lori isn't crying because she is hurt; she's crying because she is under *conviction*." I wasn't sure what my mother meant by conviction, but I realized there was another reason for my tears. I wasn't hurt. I brushed off the dirt, dried my tears, and thought, I'll just ignore my feelings and they'll go away.

The next day, as I played on the campgrounds with my friends, I pushed thoughts of sin out of my mind. When the evening service began, I decided again to play in the dirt and look for coins. When the evangelist began to preach, however, my heart continued to wage the war declared the previous night.

As my mind flip-flopped I reasoned, Why did I need to be born again when I knew about Jesus and obeyed his teachings? I soon learned that human knowledge and actions are as filthy rags to the Lord unless God cleanses and fills our hearts with the Holy Spirit. That night, when I realized my sins had crucified Christ, my heart screamed, "I need Christ!"

When the evangelist invited those who wanted to accept Jesus as their Savior to bow at the altar and pray, I jumped up and rushed toward the altar. I knelt down and began to weep and pray. Dad and Mom came forward to pray with me and instructed me how to pray the sinner's prayer. I told Jesus I was sorry for my sin and asked for forgiveness. In a childlike way, I promised to live for Jesus and I asked him to take up residence in my heart. A beautiful sense of freedom flooded my soul. On that day I exchanged my back-burner, "inherited" religion for a front-burner relationship with Jesus Christ. Through a single act of faith I became a Christian and began a lifelong process of serving the Lord.

The following summer I attended vacation Bible school and the words of one of my teachers caught my attention. "If you want to grow as a Christian," she said, "you need to pray and study your Bible." I had heard the words before, but this time they created within me a desire to get serious about my devotions on a daily basis.

Later, during junior high school I caught a spiritual disease called rebellion. I sassed my parents, picked on my brothers, and joined my peers with the attitude that said, "I'll have my way or else!" I tried to prevent my defiance from extending into my relationship with God. I refused to smoke, drink alcohol, or do drugs with my friends. I did not want to disappoint God. My family members, however, received the brunt of my bratty behavior.

One Sunday Dad warned me I had only fifteen minutes to get dressed before our evening service started. I did look gross. I was wearing an old sweatshirt and ragged jeans, and my hair was a mess. I stalled until time for church and then decided, I'm not going. It's time I take charge of my life. About ten minutes later I could imagine my dad's eyes searching the congregation for me. What would he do when he missed me? I wondered. I spent another ten minutes debating what to do.

Twenty minutes after the service started I walked into the sanctuary, sweatshirt, tattered jeans, and all. I sat on the back row and talked to a friend about a recent movie I had seen.

"Shh," my friend said. "Your dad is looking at us."

"I don't care," I said and continued talking about the movie.

My friend nudged me. "Your dad is walking toward us."

Dad came to the back row and looked me straight in the eye. "Lori," he said in a firm tone of voice, "go home, change clothes, come back, and sit in the front row."

Humiliated, I made a quick exit. When I returned, I was so fiery mad that I stomped down the center aisle, sat down on the front row, and glared at my father through the rest of the service.

When the service ended and we were alone, Dad said to me in a soft and compassionate voice, "Lori, I'm sorry I embarrassed you, but I did not know what else to do. You threw me a challenge and I had to meet it head-on."

I could feel my father's love for me as he explained that my attitude should reflect my relationship with Christ. The experience impressed me, but the real turning point in my spiritual life came some time later.

Another time during my rebellious years my dad came home and found Mom crying in frustration. "I've had it with Lori," she said. "She's wrecking our family."

Dad went into his office and came out with some construction paper. He handed me a piece of paper and said, "Go to your room and make a card to take to Mrs. Stalnaker. I'm going to visit her and you're going along."

I grabbed the paper, went into my room, and slammed the door. Out of spite, I folded the paper in a haphazard manner, ripped a flower from a magazine, pasted it on the front of the card, and scribbled inside, "I love you. Lori."

Mrs. Stalnaker was pleased to see Dad, but she directed most of her attention toward me. That embarrassed me. I wished my heart had been full of love instead of hate when I wrote those words.

When I gave Mrs. Stalnaker the card, tears filled her eyes, and she said, "You are such a blessing. You are the sweetest girl I know."

Wow! Her words hit me as hard as if Jesus himself had pointed his finger at me and said, "You hypocrite!"

I went home and poured out my heart to God. Tears now accompanied my plea for forgiveness. "Jesus, I want to quit making people miserable and start making them happy. Please help me," I prayed.

Another turning point in my spiritual life occurred when I was in high school and would go with my father to visit people in the hospital. During one visit Dad talked to me about being totally committed to Christ. "Dad, Jesus will always be a part of my life," I said.

I shall never forget my father's response. "Lori, Jesus doesn't want *part* of you; he wants *all* of you. He will not settle for a slice of your life; he wants complete control." Since that time I have continued to discover ways I can give more of myself to God. Like

Paul the apostle, "I die [to self] every day!" (1 Corinthians 15:31).

I share my personal experiences with you because I hope my testimony will encourage you to examine your relationship with God. Good people sometimes ask me if I think they are going to hell. I reply, "Let me tell you how you get to heaven. Then you can decide whether you are going to heaven or to hell."

The Bible shows us the way to heaven. Lloyd J. Ogilvie stressed the importance of following the biblical steps to salvation when he said, "Many church people are trying to live a life they have never begun." In light of this, here are some simple steps to help you begin your spiritual life.

Acknowledge Your Need of a Savior

Growing up in the church can give you a head start in gaining knowledge of the Christian life. Sometimes, though, a religious background can hinder an individual from personally experiencing God. It can nurture an easy intellectual acceptance of important biblical teachings without allowing the gospel message or the person of Jesus to affect the condition of the heart.

During a revival meeting when the evangelist invited persons to come forward to receive Jesus as Savior, the pianist slipped from the piano bench to kneel at the altar. The young woman in her twenties said to the evangelist, "All my life people have thought of me as a Christian. I thought I was a Christian, too; but tonight I realize I am not." Her work as a church pianist and as a Sunday school teacher could not make up for her lack of a personal relationship with Jesus Christ.

Perhaps a look at the biblical story of Nicodemus will point out the difference between human excellence and righteousness through Jesus. Nicodemus was as good as he could get on his own. As a religious leader he was on top of the heap, so to speak. But he was not satisfied in his soul. The presence of God in Jesus attracted the great scholar, and Nicodemus could not stay away. Nicodemus may not have been able to identify what was missing from his life, but he knew Jesus had the answer.

If you remember, Jesus did not tell Nicodemus to go to

church, clean up his act, or start doing this and stop doing that. There was nothing Nicodemus could do to earn God's love. Jesus simply said, "Very truly, I tell you, no one can see the kingdom of God without being born from above" (John 3:3). Only a spiritual new birth could make Nicodemus whole and satisfied.

In contrast to Nicodemus, Zacchaeus stands out as an overt sinner. No one respected the tax collector who made himself rich by raising taxes and pocketing the excess. Yet Jesus received Zacchaeus as readily as he received Nicodemus. Zacchaeus and Nicodemus shared the same spiritual need. They were both sinners. "There is no distinction, since all have sinned and fall short of the glory of God" (Romans 3:22–23).

Sin affects all of us. Adam's sin plunged the world into a hopeless predicament. We are born without a personal relationship with God and, as sinners, we deserve death. Scripture reminds us that "the wages of sin is death, but the free gift of God is eternal life in Christ Jesus our Lord" (Romans 6:23).

Recognize Jesus as Your Savior

Jesus is the only remedy for sin. "There is salvation in no one else, for there is no other name under heaven given among mortals by which we must be saved" (Acts 4:12).

Jesus has the authority to forgive sin because he is the Son of God (Romans 8:3). With no sin in his own life, Jesus willingly shed his blood for our sins (1 Peter 1:19). God completed the plan of salvation by raising Jesus from the dead (Romans 4:25). Belief that leads to salvation requires more than affirming Jesus was a good person, or even a holy man. We must affirm Jesus was the divine Son of God who fulfilled all the Old Testament promises.

Act on Your Convictions

As important as it is to believe in Christ as your Savior, intellectual assent is not enough for salvation. "Even the demons believe—and shudder" (James 2:19). Realizing our lost condition will not save us unless we follow through with appropriate action. Failing to act on our convictions would be like going to the doctor for a serious illness and then refusing to follow the doctor's order to regain health.

The sickness of sin calls for an old-fashioned dose of repentance. "Repent therefore, and turn to God so that your sins may be wiped out" (Acts 3:19). Repentance is ongoing and involves change. It includes a turning away from anything that stands between God and us. It is through this change, this renewing of our minds that stems from repentance, that we become new creatures in Christ. The nature of change will vary according to the circumstances and the personalities of all individuals.

Some people show emotion more easily than others. Salvation, however, does not depend upon emotions. It is God's free gift to us when we respond in faith.

God designed the plan of salvation, Jesus paid the price with his death, and the Holy Spirit invites us to accept Jesus as Savior. We need only pray a simple but sincere prayer such as, "Lord Jesus, I need you. I believe you are the Son of God and I accept you as my Savior. Forgive my sins and come into my life. Amen."

Believe God

God does not issue birth certificates when you experience this new birth. You are born into the family of God through faith; and by faith you believe God will fulfill promises of Scripture.

If you do desire physical evidence of a spiritual experience, you have the right to create your own spiritual birth certificate. You might write the information in your Bible or make up a certificate to place in your Bible. Include your name, the date you accepted Christ as Savior, and the prayer you prayed. You might also get encouragement in the future by writing out a Bible verse that God used to speak to you. Possible passages include Romans 10:9 or 1 John 1:9. One of my favorite passages reads, "This is the testimony: God gave us eternal life, and this life is in his Son. Whoever has the Son has life; whoever does not have the Son of God does not have life" (1 John 5:11–12).

Even if you do not need a new birth certificate to support the reality of your Christian experience, keeping a journal might prove valuable in your spiritual growth. Not only is it good to remind yourself of your spiritual roots, you have a tool to send Satan on the run when doubts arise. Tell Satan to butt out of your life in the name of Jesus and quote the scripture you have claimed. Satan can't stand up to that combination of power.

Times of Refreshing

When you bring Christ to the front burner of your life, you achieve a major victory. Your next challenge is to retain the victory. From time to time most Christians feel their walk with the Lord needs a jump start.

We can recognize the need for spiritual renewal by asking ourselves questions like these: Has my spiritual life gone sour? Does talking about my faith excite me? Do I possess the joy of salvation? Do worldly activities that once appalled me now seem okay?

When God becomes less important than at any time previously, we need to recommit our lives to Jesus Christ. When Peter preached repentance and a turning away from sin, he also promised "that times of refreshing [would] come from the presence of the Lord" (Acts 3:20).

We renew our commitments to God the same way we were born again. John instructed those who had lost their first love to repent and do the works they did at first (Revelation 2:5). Admit your need to be restored to spiritual wholeness. Ask God to forgive you for a lukewarm attempt to live the Christian life. Confess any actions or attitudes that are wrong. Ask God to send the Holy Spirit in a fresh, new way. Open your heart to God's Spirit and seek to live daily in the Spirit.

Of course spiritual renewal will not take place in our lives unless we follow our repentance with action. We must correct the condition that caused our mediocre experience. We will explore several ways to do this in later chapters. For now, let us say regular church attendance is a good place to begin. You can also eliminate unhealthy relationships that drag you down spiritually. Establish new friendships that help nurture your relationship with God. Find spiritual strength and support in a small group in your local congregation. Open yourself up to the group. Share prayer concerns with others and study the Bible together.

In order to have a front-burner religion, pray the following prayer. It would be helpful for you to find another person and pray the prayer together.

God, thank you for sending your Son as a sacrifice for my sins. Thank you for forgiving my sins. I accept with gratitude your forgiveness and your gift of eternal life. You know how easy it is to allow wrong attitudes, selfish interests, and human weakness to hinder my relationship with you. I offer myself in total surrender to you. Lord, surround me with your love and pour out your Spirit on me in a fresh, new way. Give me power to begin a dynamic, victorious walk with you. I pray in Jesus' name. Amen.

***

Write a testimony that describes your relationship with God. Include how you became aware of your need for God and how you responded.

_____

_____

_____

_____

_____

_____

_____

_____

_____

If you feel your Christian experience has grown stale, write out your personal prayer for a renewed commitment with God.

_____

_____

_____

_____

_____

_____

_____

_____

_____

Chapter 3
Heaven's Advice Column

John has been a Christian for two years but he lacks confidence in planning his future. He keeps asking himself, "Does God understand me? Do I understand God? Does God know what I'm all about?"

Kathi takes her Christian commitment seriously but she sometimes feels as if she is going around in circles trying to zero in on the direction God would have her take. "If I knew God's will for my life, I'd move full speed ahead," Kathi says. As she fumbles around in confusion, Kathi loses some of her zeal for the Lord.

Discerning God's will can be a major trouble spot in the Christian life. Not everyone has confidence in this area.

Before we try to discern God's will, however, let's think about who God is. A verse of Scripture often came to my mind when I traveled between Phoenix and Los Angeles. Isaiah wrote, "Who has measured the waters in the hollow of his hand / and marked off the heavens with a span?" (40:12). I tried to imagine how long it would take me to measure the three hundred miles between those cities with the span of my hand. The thought of such an undertaking boggles my mind, but God can stretch forth one hand and measure the entire universe! Wow!

This same God will allow you and me to know the will of God! Doesn't that excite you? You can know the mind of God (1 Corinthians 2:16)! Your heart, your will, can be in such complete harmony with God's will that they are one. We don't have to wonder if God's gonna go poof and disappear. God doesn't say, "See, I'm over here, but you guys are over there," in some sort of hide and seek game. God wants us to know the will of God.

Still, God doesn't place that will on billboards and seldom speaks to us in an audible voice. We need to take the initiative in knowing and learning God's will for our lives. God says, "I want you to seek hard after me. I'm not going to give you everything on a silver platter. I want you to search for me with all your heart. Seek me and you will find me" (Jeremiah 29:13, paraphrased).

A remote harbor in Italy can be reached only through a narrow channel lined with rough rocks. Many ships have been lost at night as the captain tried to navigate the vessel to port. The maritime authorities decided to install three special lights to direct ships through the rough channel. The captains of the ships, however, do not direct their ships from one light to another. Rather, they align all three lights in their vision so they appear to be one guiding light leading to the harbor.

In much the same way, we discern God's will for our lives. God has given us certain lights to guide our way. If we bring them into harmony with one another, we can walk confidently, joyfully, and excitedly in the center of God's will every day of our lives. That's exciting truth! That's wonderful! We need not wonder or waver or be confused. We are people of light!

God's Beacon Light

Now let's talk about discerning God's will. Simply put, God's will is scriptural, mandatory, and absolute! That means that God's will as revealed in the Bible is compulsory—no compromise permitted!

In Acts 20:27 Paul wrote, "I did not shrink from declaring to you the whole purpose of God." Again in Ephesians 5:17 Paul wrote, "Do not be foolish, but understand what the will of the Lord is." These two passages promise we can discover the bulk of God's will through the Bible.

The following exercise will help you visualize where in our lives God's will is revealed. On a sheet of typing paper draw a large circle. This is the core circle. In the very center of the circle write "God's Mandatory Will." Next, make eight sections in the circle as if you were cutting a pie. Each section represents God's specific will, required for everyone. Read the typical situations written as letters to "Heaven's Advice Column." From the responses, write the key word(s) and the scripture reference in each of the eight sections of the circle.

1. Floundering in Florida—I was raised in a Christian home but I got off track and really blew it. Now I'm sorry, but I feel funny around Christians. Maybe *salvation* isn't for me.

Dear Floundering,
Second Peter 3:9 clearly states that God wants everyone to be saved; and salvation is through Jesus Christ.

2. Lonely in Louisiana—I make friends quickly but can't seem to hang onto them. As soon as I start making headway, my friends tune me out. Am I supposed to be a loner?

Dear Lonely,
Have you failed to establish *loving relationships*? Read and start practicing 1 Corinthians 13.

3. Busy in Boston—I'd like to spend more time reading my Bible, but I don't seem to find enough time now for my homework, part-time job, and drama club.

Dear Busy,
Try getting up fifteen minutes earlier to read from Psalm 119. Notice the chapter promises hope, strength, truth, understanding, and purity from God's Word. As a Christian, won't you adjust your schedule to make time for *Bible reading*?

4. Self-sufficient in South Carolina—Since I don't have any major problems, I don't bother God with trivial matters. Why would God be interested in hearing from me?

Dear Self-sufficient,
It's unbelievable, but God can run the universe and still have time for every concern. Isn't that wonderful? Besides, 1 Thessalonians 5:17 clearly commands, "Pray without ceasing." Through *prayer* we can know and remain in God's will.

5. Isolated in Idaho—I live a long way from a local congrega-

tion and don't have a very good car. I believe I can be a Christian at home just as well as in church; so I don't go.

Dear Isolated,

According to Hebrews 10:25, we all need the *Christian fellowship* that a local congregation provides. Come together and exhort one another.

6. Pressured in Pennsylvania—I've been dating this Christian guy for more than a year. He says we've known each other long enough to have sex. Since we can't get married for two or three years, maybe he's right. I don't want to lose him.

Dear Pressured,

A Christian guy cannot disregard God's call to *sexual purity*. First Thessalonians 4:3 begins with strong language, "This is the will of God ... that you abstain from fornication."

7. Crushed in California—I used to be a happy Christian when I thought I would go to college on an athletic scholarship. Since an accident ended my dream, my happiness has turned to bitterness.

Dear Crushed,

I'm deeply sorry about your accident and I want you to know that God shares your pain. Don't spend your life in bitterness, though, because that is not God's will. Offer *thanksgiving* to God for life! First Thessalonians 5:18 reads "Give thanks in all circumstances; for this is the will of God in Christ Jesus for you."

8. Timid in Tennessee—I accepted Jesus as my Savior when I was ten years old. Now that I'm in high school, I don't let anyone know I'm a Christian for fear I'll be ridiculed.

Dear Timid,

From Matthew 28:19 we learn the importance of *witnessing*. Matthew 5:11–12 will help you overcome your fear.

God speaks to us through the Bible. You can find a Bible verse that will help you understand God's will in any situation. When you find one that applies to you, write it on an index card. Think of your collection of cards as calling cards from God. Carry one or two in your pocket. When you're out running errands or waiting at a check-out counter, take out a card for a quick review. You'll be surprised how quickly God's light shines in and through you.

Personal Options

As revealed in Scripture, God's will is the same for everyone. God requires us all to live by certain standards, but there are some personal decisions we must make that may be different from someone else's decision. Where should I go to college? What vocation should I choose? Will I marry? If so, how will I find the right person to marry? These are tough issues—too important to take lightly.

At one time in my life I wished I could have turned to Jude 2:5 and read, "Lori Marvel shall marry Kurt Salierno." Yeah, I know Jude has only one chapter and that's the point. I had the freedom to make a choice! That's exciting!

Guess what? If you already practice the truths found in the core circle exercise, then you can do whatever you want with your personal decisions. Wow! That's a strong statement, and a lot depends on the word *if.*

So—do I marry Kurt or do I stay single? "If your life is in the center of God's will," a pastor said to me, "you can marry Kurt and be in God's will or you can stay single and be in God's will."

After Kurt and I made our decision to marry, we went to my dad. Kurt took a straightforward approach. "Dad, I'm going to marry your daughter. I want to know if it's okay with you."

Maybe Dad came on strong because he didn't know if Kurt was telling or asking. "Wait a minute," he said. "Have you thought this thing through?"

That was my cue to speak up with my usual sound reasoning. "Think what through, Dad? I'm twenty-one and Kurt's twenty-two. We both love the Lord and we're excited. I think he's cute. He thinks I'm cute. What more is there to think about?"

"Hold on, Lori. You're going into ministry. Kurt's going into ministry. Will one of you want to live in Oregon and the other one in Indiana?"

"What are you getting at, Dad?"

Dad explained that not many congregations can afford to hire two people at the same time. Even if they did, they probably wouldn't hire a husband and wife team. When Dad finished giving us the third degree, we both realized there was more to think about.

We sat quietly for a few moments, and then Kurt said, "Dad, I hear what you're saying, but we're going to go for it! We believe God will guide us and provide for us."

We married and moved to Seattle, Washington, where I finished college. After working in a day nursery for nine months, I began to get fidgety because I wanted to be in ministry. I talked to Kurt, and he said, "Lori, just trust God."

Kurt and I began to pray and wait on God. One Saturday morning I answered the phone and heard the caller ask, "Would you and your husband be interested in interviewing for jobs as co-youth ministers?" We had prayed to hear those words.

I tried to play it cool, but I couldn't hold down the excitement I felt. Before Kurt and I had a chance to talk about it, the phone rang again. A similar offer came from Indiana. In fact, the pastor said, "I believe it's God's will that you come to this church."

After we interviewed for both positions, we talked to Kurt's boss, the pastor in Seattle. "It's God's will that you stay here," he said.

"Kurt, someone has the wires crossed from God," I said when we got home. "How can we be three places at once?"

As Kurt and I prayed about our decision, we realized it was God's will for all three churches to have enthusiastic youth ministers, but we had the freedom to choose where we wanted to go.

Isn't that beautiful? It is our privilege to choose what is right for us if our lives are in the center of God's will.

God's Harbor Lights

To complete your diagram representing God's will, draw a larger circle around the core circle. Label this circle "God's Guidance." This represents direction for your life when God has not been specific. Include the Bible reference Proverbs 3:5–6,

"Trust in the LORD with all your heart, / and do not rely on your own insight. / In all your ways acknowledge him / and he will make straight your paths."

Draw three lights in this larger circle. These lights represent ways God will guide you in your personal decisions. Remember, you're looking at life through a peephole. God sees the whole parade from beginning to end—from before you were born until after you die.

Label the first light *divine impressions*. These are strong feelings that come to you as a result of prayer. As you consistently pray for direction, you will learn to recognize God's voice. You will learn to distinguish that faint whisper from your own voice and from Satan's voice as you submit your life and work to God.

In my first year of college I decided to conduct an experiment. During my morning prayer I said, "Lord, I'd like for you to give me the name of someone I should pray for." I got my pencil and waited. The name came and I wrote it down, but I did not know Pam Baxter (not her real name).

At first I thought it was exciting to pray for someone I didn't know, but after a couple of months I began to question God. Who was Pam Baxter? Was my prayer doing any good? God said, "Just keep on praying."

One day I walked down the hall and saw a name on the door of one of the dorm rooms that caused my heart to flutter. There really was a Pam Baxter. I started praying harder than ever, but I didn't want to meet her because I didn't know what to say to her.

Another two months went by before Pam Baxter came to find me. "Lori, I'm not sure why, but I've got to talk to you tonight," she said. I went to her room and she told the worst life story I had ever heard. The hate and bitterness she harbored in her heart had led to depression and attempted suicide.

When she finished her story Pam said, "I may never acknowledge your presence again. I have never told this to anyone, but for some reason I had to tell you, and I'm not sure why."

I went to my room and fell beside my bed. "God," I said, "will I ever, ever realize how great you are?"

I heard from Pam once after she left school. She asked me if I still prayed for her. "Pam," I said, "this morning I asked God to spill the Holy Spirit on your heart that you might come to the saving knowledge of who God is."

She said, "Lori, I want to tell you something. I may never accept your God. I may never become a Christian, but I want you to know that you are the only person on this earth who cares whether I live or die because you pray."

I hope that someday my prayers will be answered for Pam Baxter, but for now at least she knows someone cares; and through that experience I learned to discern God's still, small voice.

Label the second guiding light *circumstances*. In his biographies of Abraham Lincoln, Carl Sandburg tells a story that illustrates how God provides guidance through circumstances.[1]

With a partner named Barry, Mr. Lincoln owned a store that was about to fail. The two men were sitting out in front of the store one day trying to figure out how they could make a go of the business when a man and his wife and children drove up in a wagon. They all looked tired and hungry.

"I have a barrel to sell," the man said. "Could you use a good barrel? It's fifty cents."

Abraham Lincoln reached into his pocket and pulled out his last fifty cents and handed it to the man because his heart was touched by their plight.

"Well, that was smart!" Barry said. "We're about to go broke, and you put your last fifty cents in an old barrel."

Disregarding the sarcasm, Mr. Lincoln said, "If we could just sell this store, pay off our debts, and have a little money left over, I would buy *Blackstone's Commentary on English Law*."

"Dream on!" Barry said. "We can't even pay the bills."

As Barry ridiculed him throughout the day, Mr. Lincoln's mood fell. Toward evening, he walked past the barrel and noticed some papers in the bottom. Under the papers, Abraham Lincoln found a book titled *Blackstone's Commentary on English Law*.

The man who would become a renowned president of the

United States of America stood looking into the heavens. Recalling his experience later Lincoln said, "A deep impression came over me that God had something for me to do and was preparing me for it. If not, why this miracle?"

The third light in the outer circle of God's guidance represents *counsel* with other Christians. "Without counsel, plans go wrong, / but with many advisers they succeed" (Proverbs 15:22). I like to suggest consulting at least three Christians who are living close to God before making an important decision. In some cases it will be helpful to talk with someone who has experience in the concern about which you seek guidance. If you're thinking about going into business, talk with someone who has a successful business. You may get a different answer from each person, but consider all ideas as you pray and search God's Word. Conflicting ideas may make your decision difficult, but wrestle with your options until you receive a sense of peace that comes from God.

As you evaluate your guiding lights, you will want to make sure that each one lines up with the central beacon light of the core circle. Any light that contradicts God's Word must be rejected. In fact, if all three guiding lights are in agreement against Scripture, the Bible still remains your final measuring stick.

For example, you receive an offer to work for Company A and another offer to work for Company B. Circumstances point to Company B because the pay is better and you need money to help your parents. In church the next Sunday the emphasis is on giving. "Wow!" you think, "if I work for Company B, I can give more to the church." That impression is still strong when you receive a call from a friend who tells you that Company B is far more solid financially than Company A. That night you have a dream in which an angel stands over your bed whispering, "Company B." That does it! On Monday morning you prepare to go to Company B to accept the offer. Then you pick up your Bible and read, "Take no part in the unfruitful works of darkness" (Ephesians 5:11). You have tried to ignore the fact that Company B has a reputation for shady deals, but God will not let you. Nothing else matters when God speaks through Scripture.

If you're living by all the truth revealed to you through

Scripture, you can count on God to guide you in the optional area. When you put together God's Word with prayer as a basis for your spiritual life, you are in powerful form! You are moving toward excellence in a dynamic fashion.

On the other hand, if you're not obedient in the compulsory areas why should God guide you in optional decisions? You must live up to what you know to be right before you will receive anything more from God.

Are you at a crossroads in your life? Do you have an important decision to make? Are you anxious about an uncertain future? With the Word of God inscribed in your heart and a prayer on your lips, look for God's harbor lights and go forth to face the unknown with confidence.

Here's a prayer to help you on your way.

God, Thank you for creating me, redeeming me, and giving me your Word to help me become the person you designed me to be. Thank you for the guidance I receive through prayer, circumstances, and through the counsel of other Christians. Help me remain submissive to your will and to practice what is right. Help me place my trust in you and not lean on my own understanding. In the precious name of Jesus I pray. Amen.

When you finish your diagram, it should look like one on the opposite page.

***

Discerning God's Will

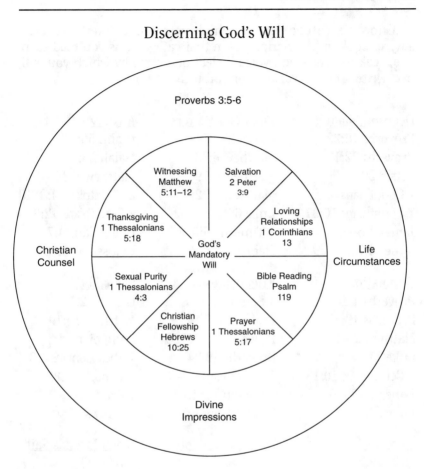

Choose a category from which you would like to receive advice. Look up the Scriptures in that category. As you read each one, seek to hear God's voice. Select one verse by which you will live, write it on a card, and commit it to memory.

Decision Making
Proverbs 15:22
Proverbs 22:1
Acts 5:29
1 Corinthians 9:19
1 Corinthians 10:31
James 1:5–6
James 4:7

Financial Matters
Psalm 37:25
Matthew 6:33
Matthew 6:19–20
Matthew 16:25
Luke 6:38
1 Timothy 6:6–8
Hebrews 13:5

Anxiety
Psalm 56:3
Isaiah 26:3
Matthew 6:34
2 Corinthians 4:8–10
2 Corinthians 12:9
Philippians 4:7
Colossians 3:15

Temptation
Proverbs 1:10
Proverbs 19:27
Matthew 26:41
Luke 11:4
1 Corinthians 10:13
James 1:14–15
James 4:7

Friendships
1 Samuel 20:17
Psalm 1:1
Proverbs 22:24–25
Proverbs 29:24
1 Corinthians 5:6–7
1 Corinthians 15:33
2 Corinthians 6:14

Sexuality
Genesis 2:18
Matthew 15:19
Philippians 4:8
1 Thessalonians 4:3–5
2 Timothy 2:22
1 Peter 2:11
Hebrews 13:4

Suffering
Psalm 23:4
John 14:1
Romans 14:8
Philippians 1:21
James 5:14
1 Peter 4:12

Drugs and Alcohol
Leviticus 10:9
Proverbs 20:1
Proverbs 23:29–32
Isaiah 5:11
Luke 21:34
Ephesians 5:18

When Friends Fail
Job 16:20
Psalm 41:9–10
Matthew 5:11–12
Matthew 10:35
Mark 14:50
Luke 17:3–4

Chapter 4
Tapping the Powerline

When I was in high school I told a friend I would return a plate to her on Wednesday night at church. She told me to wait until the following Sunday because she didn't attend church on Wednesday night. When she told me why, I wasn't sure I heard her right.

"All they do is pray on Wednesday night," she repeated.

Her remark disturbed me so much I went home to my bedroom, fell on my knees, and cried out, "God, help the church!"

I asked my dad why our church was filled on Sunday morning yet only a handful of people attend prayer meeting.

Dad shook his head as he answered, "Lori, I've been in the ministry for twenty-one years, and that question has pounded my brain day after day after day." He paused and then added, "Maybe, just maybe, prayer is not entertaining enough for them."

When Christians fall on their knees, or even pray in their hearts, they are tapping power, love, and all that God is in such a way that God becomes a real part of their lives. Prayer totally transforms us physically, emotionally, and spiritually in such a way that we influence everyone around us. With that kind of motivation to pray, do we need to be entertained? Does God need to tickle our fancy before we'll pray?

The fifteenth chapter of John is one of my favorite passages. It points out the by-products of an active prayer life. Verse 4 reads, "Abide in me as I abide in you." Other versions use the word *remain.* One version, the Living Bible, reads, "Take care to live in me, and let me live in you." An exchange of lives is just about as intimate as two people can get.

Jesus spoke these words to his disciples just before he died. He wanted them to know that the intimacy he had shared with them could continue. The disciples could remain aware of Jesus' presence if they would allow him to live through them.

Jesus wanted his disciples to abide in him in order that they might bear much fruit. Fruitful Christians *glorify God* and *demonstrate God's love in the world.* Jesus also wanted his disciples to experience the fullness of joy that comes through an intimate relationship with him.

When I lived in Louisiana, a woman in the church invited our family to lunch—a rare occasion for the Marvel family. As we drove along in our green Pontiac, Dad glanced in the rearview mirror at my two brothers and me in the back seat. "Lori, Jerry, and Bob," Dad said, "Mrs. Monasco has been kind enough to invite us for lunch. Would you please behave and be polite?"

"Gotcha!" Bob said.

"No problem," Jerry said.

In response to my silence, Dad said, "Lori, do you hear me?"

"Yeah," I said, meaning that I had heard with my ears but not necessarily with my heart.

As I watched Mrs. Monasco remove the golden tableware when we finished eating, I thought she must be the richest woman in Louisiana. When she placed a bowl of fruit in the center of the table, I spied grapes as big as plums. "Before I leave here, one of those grapes is going to be in my mouth," I promised myself. I wasn't sure how I could pull it off under my parents' watchful eyes, but I would give it a good try.

When everyone settled in the living room, I edged my way to the table and plucked the biggest grape I could find and plopped it in my mouth. I began to chew and chew and chew.

Mom looked up and said, "Lori, what do you have in your mouth?"

I managed to maneuver the grape to one side and mumble, "A fake grape!"

As Christians, do we sometimes present ourselves to the world as fake grapes? Do we look good but turn out to be nothing but plastic when the world takes a bite of us? If we fail to be fruitful, we also fail to glorify God and prove to the world we are Jesus' disciples.

How can we abide in Christ? The only way we can abide in Christ, the only way we can bear fruit, the only way we can know God intimately is through prayer. We cannot move toward spiritual maturity, much less excellence, without prayer.

Obstacles to Prayer

If prayer is important, why don't Christians spend more time praying? I believe Christians fail to pray for two major reasons.

First, we allow ourselves to become too *busy*. Our schedules pile up with activities until we have no room left for God.

You might say, "Lori, do you remember what it was like to be a student? I spend four hours each day in class and homework requires another four hours. Then I work my job a couple hours each day and eight hours on Saturday. That's sixty hours a week! Add to that some time I need for myself. I watch a little television, go on a date or two, hang out with the crowd, and spend a few hours on the tennis court. When do you expect me to find time to pray?"

Yes, I do remember when my schedule was packed to the max, but do you want to know something? My schedule is still packed. At least three things pop up to compete for every single open slot on my calendar. If I'm going to pray, I'll have to do it at an inconvenient time because a convenient time will never come.

One day Jesus stopped at the home of Mary and Martha. Mary sat at the feet of Jesus listening to what he said while Martha prepared a meal. After a while, Martha got so fiery mad she complained to Jesus.

"The Lord answered her, 'Martha, Martha, you are worried and distracted by many things; there is need of only one thing. Mary has chosen the better part, which will not be taken away from her' " (Luke 10:41–42). Perhaps Jesus would have preferred a donut and a cup of coffee in order to enjoy the companionship of both Mary and Martha.

Mary teaches us the *importance of prayer* in communion with God. We don't pray because prayer isn't important. In the church, we tend to substitute programs for prayer. We get so busy *doing* Christian things that we forget to *be* with God.

Do you realize we can fulfill our destinies only through prayer? Prayer is our lifeline. God created us in order to have fellowship with us. How can we maintain a casual attitude toward prayer when we are so important to God?

Do you know how I know Christians fail to place enough importance on prayer? Because I fail myself. I must keep reminding myself I can do nothing apart from Christ living in me. Without Jesus, I will fall flat on my face, and he will not continue to abide with me unless I spend time in his presence.

Aids to Prayer

Okay, you're enthusiastic about prayer and ready to go. When you start to pray, though, you run into a roadblock, like two-year-old Christy experienced.

When a family problem came up, Grandma said, "Christy, we need to pray about this."

"Right now?" Christy said.

"Yes."

Christy bowed her head and said, "Dear Jesus ..." Then she raised her eyes and turned to Grandma. "Now what?"

If you run out of words to pray, I'd like to offer four suggestions to help you develop an intimate relationship with God.

First, *find quality time*. Don't give God your leftover time. Give God your prime time when you're at your best. If you're most alert in the morning, give God time in the morning. If you're a night person, give God time in the evening. If you really get going about noon, give God your lunch break. Allow God to break in on your thoughts throughout the day, but set aside some specific time for just the two of you to be together.

Second, *resist the devil like crazy*. As soon as you start to pray, Satan will come on strong. Thoughts will pop in your mind. What do you suppose will be on the test tomorrow? Was there a hidden meaning in Mary's remark? Don't forget to call the pastor to volunteer for the nursery. Satan will use any excuse to keep you from praying because he knows more about the power of prayer than most Christians. Don't let Satan get away with distracting your mind! And don't feel guilty when you fail. Keep on trying!

Third, *feed your soul on spiritual food daily*. How would you like to try an experiment for a week? Eat a big meal after church on Sunday and then go without food until the next Sunday. Can you imagine crawling into church and begging an usher to help you to your seat? Of course not. You'd veto that idea in a hurry.

But are you living on that kind of a spiritual diet? If God suddenly transformed your physical body into a spiritual body, what would it look like? Would you vanish like the wind? Would you be so weak that someone would have to carry you to a spiritual hospital? Maybe you'd be flabby because you take in from God but you never serve or exercise your gifts. The right diet and exercise for your spiritual body will count more in the end than keeping in shape physically.

Fourth, *follow an explicit prayer plan*. From various prayers recorded in the Bible (including the prayer Jesus taught his disciples), we learn there are different kinds of prayer. These examples of effective prayer provide us with a pattern for talking with God.

Steps in Prayer

Whether it comes from David, Nehemiah, Hezekiah, or Jesus, prayer began with *praise*. Praise is complimenting God for who God is—not for the blessings received. The mere fact that God is God warrants our praise. During worship we sense God's presence and unconditional love. That's my favorite part of prayer—letting God love me. I feel secure, overjoyed. Sometimes I get so excited I jump up and yell, "Hot dog!" because God's love feels so good.

Confession comes next. Confession is often painful but necessary to bring about a sense of oneness between God and you. Not only does confession involve asking forgiveness for failures that you recognize, it also consists of allowing God to reveal to you anything else in your life that is wrong. With a clean slate between you and God, you're ready to move ahead in your worship experience.

Soak your mind with God's Word. During your prayer time as well as throughout the day, reflect on what God is saying to you through Scripture. If you've ever visited a farm, you've probably watched a cow chew her cud. While a cow lacks glamour as a role model, she can show us how to meditate on God's Word. We read it, we chew it, we chew it some more, we swallow, and then we bring it back up to start the process all over again. We play detective and investigate the passage, comparing it with other passages. We ask questions and our flesh tingles with excitement when we find the answers.

An unselfish prayer includes *intercession*—praying for other people. A higher form of intercessory prayer goes beyond the needs of family and friends to include the nerds and even your enemies. If you really want to reach beyond yourself and make a difference, pray for a revival.

One summer I worked at a church as youth minister. Carey and Tommy seemed to be leaders in the church so I asked them to tell me about the congregation.

"I've been here almost eight years, and you'll never find a better bunch of people," Carey said. "They'll have you over for dinner and be as nice as they can, but, Lori, they're dead."

Tommy agreed. "I don't know of anyone who has gone to the altar in the last six or seven years," he said.

I wasn't too keen on spending the next three months among a bunch of spiritually dead people and I asked Carey and Tommy to help me.

"What did you have in mind?" they asked.

"Meet me at my place next Tuesday at six o'clock in the morning," I said.

Neither Carey nor Tommy went wild over my idea, but they grudgingly agreed to show up.

On Tuesday morning I looked at Tommy's sleepy eyes and

Carey's eyes without her makeup and wondered what it would take to bring about a revival.

"Well, what are we going to do?" Carey said.

"We're going to pray. We're going to pray for the preacher. We're going to pray for the pianist. We're going to pray for the organist. We're going to ask God to bring life to this church."

When we finished praying, Tommy said, "I didn't feel anything."

My faith wasn't strong enough to be contagious but I said, "Be here next Tuesday."

Three or four weeks went by and enthusiasm was dwindling. I knew we couldn't survive on negative enthusiasm so I said, "Okay, you guys, we're going to pray with fire this morning."

"How do you pray with fire?" Tommy asked.

"Ask God to ignite us with the Holy Spirit in church next Sunday morning," I said.

When Carey prayed, she said, "Lord, I pray that something different will happen this Sunday that didn't happen last Sunday."

That didn't challenge my faith because nothing had happened the Sunday before.

Tommy prayed, "Lord, I've never done this before, but I pray fire on the preacher's head."

When Sunday came, major disappointments punctured our high expectations. On Tuesday I said, "We're not giving up! Still praying fire, Tommy?"

"Well, maybe I'll pray for a little flame."

Later in the week I talked to the pastor. I asked him to join us to pray for the power of God in our services. He didn't think he could work it into his schedule but said he wanted to affirm what we were doing.

The Sunday finally came when one person responded to the altar call. Carey pinched me so hard I thought I would bleed. The next Sunday the altar was filled.

Tommy said, "We're going to get together at 4:30 next week."

The church began to grow. The youth group went from five kids to fifteen to thirty. We kept on praying and the services got more dynamic. One Tuesday while we were praying, we heard a knock on the door. The pastor joined us to testify that his faith had been renewed in the power of intercessory prayer.

Petition is the most common form of prayer. In fact, some people limit their entire prayer life to "Gimmee, gimmee, gimmee." While God is not a year-around Santa Claus, Jesus taught his disciples to ask for their daily bread. It is our privilege to depend on God for all our needs. Jesus said, "If you abide in me, and my words abide in you, ask for whatever you wish, and it will be done for you" (John 15:7). That sounds almost like a blank-check provision, but we must meet the requirement before we can claim the promise. If we abide in Jesus, we will learn to desire what God desires for us.

Only an ill-mannered person would leave a party without thanking the host or hostess. If we leave God's presence without *giving thanks*, we become spiritual brats. Christ's words "Apart from me you can do nothing" (John 15:5) help us to realize our indebtedness to God. The concept of nothing deprives us of the ability to move, to breathe, or to think. Life itself depends on the continued goodness of God.

An exercise in thanksgiving benefits us at the same time it pleases God. When we tell God how grateful we are, God spills the praise back on us and our joy is full. It is impossible to be miserable and full of thanksgiving at the same time.

At first, following a formula may make prayer seem more mechanical than spiritual. Don't be discouraged because you feel awkward. If words don't come, that's okay too. The Bible reminds us, "We do not know how to pray as we ought, but that very Spirit intercedes with sighs too deep for words" (Romans 8:26). The Holy Spirit will translate your emotions into communion that flows between you and God.

Jesus took his burden to Gethsemane alone, but he desired the prayerful support of his disciples. Three times he returned to the disciples, hoping to receive a word of encouragement. Three times he found them sleeping. Will he find you sleeping? Will he say to you, "Could you not keep awake one hour?" (Mark 14:37).

Will you refuse to allow anything to take the place of the time that God desires with you? Without an intimate relationship with the Lord, you cannot bear fruit, testify to the world, glorify God, or be a person of joy. Only by abiding in Christ, by communing with God in prayer, can you become a person of excellence!

Here's a prayer to help you commune with God.

Almighty God, I speak your name in awe and reverence because of who you are. You are Creator, Redeemer, Friend, the Source of all life. I feel insignificant in your presence, Lord, especially as I recognize my failures. Forgive me for the times I have allowed anything but you to take first place in my life. Help me fulfill my destiny by abiding in you. Thank you for your love and for the privilege of knowing you. In Jesus' name I pray. Amen.

***

You can chart the progress of your prayer life by keeping a journal. To get started, purchase a notebook and set up three columns as follows. Write on only one side of each page.

Date of request	Nature of request	Date answered

Some prayer requests will be ongoing while others will be short term. For example, prayer for the salvation of another person will continue until he or she accepts Christ, but prayer for help on a final exam will end when you take the test.

As prayers are answered, write out sentences that offer praise to God on the back of your prayer journal sheets. When you get discouraged, review how God has already worked in your life and take heart.

When a situation calls for additional power, try the following exercise along with your regular routine.

Cut a piece of paper in an egg shape. Write out a prayer that describes your most urgent request and place the paper in your Bible. The egg shape symbolizes the time it may take to "hatch." In the Bible, the egg is covered by God's Word. Keep praying about your request as you wait for God to act.

Chapter 5
Alone in a Barren Land

During World War I a concert pianist in Europe made frequent appearances in Nazi territory. Before each performance, the pianist faced his audience and recognized God as the source of his talent. He further requested that all who were touched by his music give the glory to God. To underscore the intensity of his devotion, he offered a prayer that God be glorified through his music.

When the Nazi officials learned about the practice, they decided to take action. A commander in the military and several soldiers entered the concert hall one night and marched forward to confront the pianist. "You will no longer honor God with your talent." The harsh voice of the commander matched the stern expression on his face. "From now on you must give no glory to God during your concerts."

The pianist stepped forward and his eyes met the cold glare of the commander. His voice was softer, but he spoke with equal passion. "That's impossible, sir. I will not allow my music to fill the air without acknowledging God to my audience."

A spark-like fire flickered in the commander's eyes. "I give you one more chance," he said. "Continue with your concerts, but you must not give glory to God."

With deep conviction ringing in his voice, the pianist said, "Sir, I cannot do otherwise."

Under the commander's orders, the soldiers seized the pianist, stretched him out on the ground, tied him down and, one by one, marched over his hands, grinding flesh and bones with their cleated boots.

When the soldiers released the pianist only stubs remained on his hands as fingers. As he stood up the commander said, "Now let us hear you play. Let us hear you glorify your God who does not exist—your God who could not keep you from this."

In a gesture of reverence, the pianist pressed his bloody right hand against his breast, and said, "You can take away my fingers. You can take away my ability to play. But you will never take away the music that vibrates in my heart. I will never play again, but the song in my soul will glorify God for as long as I live!"

Storm Warnings

New Christians may wonder what kind of guarantee God gives them. Even mature Christians may ask what kind of warranty goes along with their Christian service. The answer? None! Absolutely none! God does not guarantee success just because you are a Christian. In fact, trouble may come to you because you are a Christian.

To add to the pain of tragedy, a sense of darkness may envelop you and plunge you into a spiritual desert. You may even feel alienated from God. Do you know where that idea comes from? Satan invented it to go with his "hit-'em-when-they're-down" philosophy. If Satan can make you believe God's finished with you, he has a better chance to defeat you.

You can even be alone in a barren land and still be in the center of God's will. You can be in the desert through no fault of your own. At times you feel God has forsaken you. That's simply a normal, natural part of the Christian experience.

Do you remember the story about Daniel (Daniel 6:10)? He knew a lions' den awaited anyone who prayed to a god other than King Darius. Yet Daniel opened his windows and prayed to God three times a day. I would have been tempted to close the windows and pray silently, but Daniel decided to openly worship God regardless of the consequences.

In another story from the Bible, King Nebuchadnezzar told three men named Shadrach, Meshach, and Abednego to bow down before a golden idol in order to escape a fiery furnace. They didn't even ask for time to think about their decision. I might have decided that would be a convenient time to tie a shoe. You know, I'm not really bowing. I'm just tying my shoe. They repeatedly refused to bow down to any image. They chose instead to trust God even if it meant death. They expected God to save them, but they said, "If not, be it known to you, O king, that we will not serve your gods and we will not worship the golden statue that you have set up" (Daniel 3:18). Wow! That kind of commitment to God will see us safely through any desert.

Tough Faith

Those of us who grow up in the church may develop a childlike faith. We learn Jesus loves us and we learn to love him. We're taught to believe God will provide for our needs and so we trust God will always provide what we need. Ours is a wonderful faith, but it may not deliver us safely through the hard tests of life.

We need not discard the faith of our childhood. In fact, we can preserve our young faith by encasing it in a tough exterior. Inside, we keep the tender spirit of Jesus, but outside we're ready to do battle with anything that would destroy our relationship with God. With stubborn conviction we say, "Lord, we'll serve you if you never bless us. We'll hang on to you no matter what."

In his letter to the Romans, Paul wrote, "I am convinced that neither death, nor life, nor angels, nor rulers, nor things present, nor things to come, nor powers, nor height, nor depth, nor anything else in all creation, will be able to separate us from the love of God" (Romans 8:38–39). In order to win against all the odds and experience life as *more* than a conqueror, you might find the following suggestions helpful.

Collect Testimonial Stones

When God caused the waters of the Jordan river to part and stand still, the Israelites crossed it on dry ground. At God's command, Joshua set up twelve stones taken from the river as a testimony to how God had delivered Israel from Egyptian bondage (Joshua 4).

God already had spared the firstborn of the Israelites when the death angel passed over Egypt (Exodus 12:12–13). For forty years, God provided both food and water as the Israelites wandered around lost in the desert. Isn't it interesting that, according to Scripture, their clothing and shoes did not wear out during that period? The testimonial stones became a symbol of celebration and a reason for worship.

When the stormy winds threaten to beat against you, remember what the Lord has done in your life. Remember the wonderful sense of freedom when you knew your sins were covered by the blood of Jesus. Every time you receive a blessing from God, mark the event with a testimonial stone.

Create your own way of representing the stones that remind you of how God has delivered you. For example, find a picture frame with a collage mat. Instead of filling it with photos, create a collage of memories. If you thought you might flunk geometry but God helped you understand new concepts, write a testimony. Record the time when a broken relationship was healed. If you haven't been a Christian long enough to build up a spiritual rock garden, draw from the experiences of others. Read the Bible. In the eleventh chapter of Hebrews you can read how Noah survived the taunts of those who thought he was crazy for building a boat on dry land. You can read how Abraham trusted God until the very moment he held a knife to his only son's throat. You can read why Moses chose hardships instead of the good life. The faith of God's people makes a difference, and faith will bring you victoriously through this life.

Recognize the Reality of Injustice

People stranded in a desert often complain, "It isn't fair. If God loves me, why do so many terrible things happen to me? Why did I lose my job? Why did I get cancer?"

Jesus never expected fairness for his followers or for himself. He warned his disciples to expect persecution and told Peter that old age would be unkind for him (John 21:18–19). Furthermore, Jesus died on the cross, an unjust end to his life. Because of what happened to Jesus on the cross, we can never again argue life should be fair. On the cross, Jesus became sin and through the cross God promises us freedom from sin, but that does not guarantee us immunity from injustice.

God is fair, but life is not always fair. If we confuse God's justice with physical life, we set ourselves up for disappointment. We run the risk of understanding faith as a bargaining tool. "God, I'll serve you as long as you come through for me." A faith based upon the necessity of social justice will crumble when the road gets rough. Christian faith centers upon a personal relationship with God, through Christ, rather than upon life's circumstances.

The theme of the Book of Job deals with the question of *why*. Why did Job lose his possessions, his health, and his family? "Confess your sins," his three friends said. Job searched his soul, but could find no sin to confess.

"You must have sinned or God would not be punishing you," his friends insisted. "He's not punishing us; so we must be doing okay." Obviously Job needed some new friends.

Suffering, questions, and accusations continued. Job anguished before God, but God was silent. Finally God spoke from a whirlwind. During the discourse God said in essence, Job, if you can figure out how to create the universe, then you will have the right to question me about my judgments. Wow! God did not answer Job's question "why?" However, God did allow Job to see a glimpse into divine character.

Preserve Your Integrity

When Job's wife urged him to curse God and die, she said, "Do you still persist in your integrity?" (Job 2:9). Job had unconditionally surrendered to God, and he intended to honor his commitment. Job said, "Though he slay me, yet will I hope in him" (Job 13:15, NIV).

To live with integrity means that nothing will hinder your allegiance to God. You will not cheat on an English exam. You will always tell the truth. You will not lie. If you marry, you will not find a new romance because your spouse commits adultery. You will remain true to God.

Some of the most disturbed people I meet tell me about their regrets. Unwise decisions from their past haunt them because they decided to let go of their integrity when life got tough. In a difficult situation they reason, "If God doesn't care about me, why should I care about God?" So they compromise their principles and let go of their allegiance to God, and their darkness grows even darker.

Glorify God

Job's loyalty during his trials proved his love for the Lord. God believed in Job, and Job did not let God down. While Job's sorrow brought God pain, the way Job handled the ordeal glorified God.

The story of a young woman I know resembles the story of Job. Rebecca's career had soared and her lifestyle matched—including a handsome husband. Unlike Job, though, Rebecca had turned away from God, living only for success in this world. Then, suddenly, her life fell apart. Within months her job, husband, and money were gone.

Alone and desperate, Rebecca developed a personal relationship with Jesus Christ. As she began to rebuild her life she experienced yet another tragedy—breast cancer. After her mastectomy, a yo-yo battle with cancer followed. She had another mastectomy, discovered she had bone cancer, and had a hip replaced. She experienced times of remission in some parts of her body only to be let down by a recurrence of cancer elsewhere.

As tragedy after tragedy continued, Rebecca imagined what she might say to God when she arrived in heaven. "God," she intended to say with the tenderness she felt even as she suffered, "why did you allow so many terrible things to happen to me while I was on earth?" Even as the questions haunted her, though, Rebecca sometimes sensed their answers.

While confined to a wheelchair, Rebecca turned her attention to helping others find Christ. Her mother and sister had spurned the gospel message while Rebecca was well. The graceful way she handled her suffering convinced her family she had something they wanted. They both accepted Christ as their Savior. Rebecca then expanded her evangelistic efforts—reaching the people who cared for her and anyone else who crossed her path. She inspired everyone who knew her; God was glorified in her life.

Unfortunately, such is not always the case. Sometimes the beauty of a spirit that triumphs above pain is missed altogether. What then?

Most people know the fame Joni Eareckson Tada achieved following the diving accident that left her a quadriplegic. Hers is a story of victory. During the moments when Joni recognizes the good that has come from her tragedy, she remembers Denise—a former hospital roommate.[2]

A cute, popular, healthy high-school senior, Denise stumbled one morning as she climbed the stairs between classes.

"Your diet's getting to you," a friend quipped.

Denise laughed off the incident and went on to class. When she got home, she went to bed because she could hardly walk. By dinnertime her legs were paralyzed. Within a short time her arms were paralyzed. Blindness followed and doctors diagnosed her illness as a rare form of multiple sclerosis that causes rapid deterioration.

In the hospital, Denise was quickly reduced to a spirit trapped in a body that could not function. Hardly able to speak, she couldn't read or watch television. During her eight-year ordeal Denise never complained, but no one noticed her patience. Her sweet spirit and faltering expressions of her love for God did not reach the masses. No one visited her except her mother and one other woman. Denise's life seemingly mattered to no one.

After Denise died, Joni thought, What a waste. As she and her friends began searching the Scriptures for an answer to their questions about Denise's suffering, they learned that the behavior of Christians affects the unseen world (Ephesians 3:10). The way God helped Denise handle her affliction caused angels to rejoice and demons to tremble.

Those who endure intense suffering enter into a fellowship with Jesus that can be duplicated no other way. They experience an opportunity to glorify God in a unique way. Paul wrote, "I want to know Christ and the power of his resurrection and the sharing of his sufferings" (Philippians 3:10).

Even as you stand in darkness, full of confusion and fear, God can work in and through you. No life need be lived in vain. You may never reach your desired goal or even the goal you think God has set. But how you handle your desert experiences is important to God because God is developing your spirituality. The end result of the process is what matters.

Keep Hope Alive

The final suggestion I offer for surviving the desert is never give up hope! You can endure a terrible today if you expect a better tomorrow. Although your circumstances may seem hopeless, God may lift your burden at a moment's notice.

On the other hand, you may be locked into a situation for life. In those cases we hinge hope on heaven. "This slight momentary affliction is preparing us for an eternal weight of glory beyond all measure" (2 Corinthians 4:17).

I think particularly of my friend Bob Frick. During the final months of his life, Bob suffered from bone cancer. In those few months, heaven became more real to him than his earthly existence. A sense of celebration accompanied the tears that flowed during his funeral. On that day, family and friends wanted to share Bob's glorious experience of meeting Jesus face to face.

Are you alone in a barren land right now? If you are, admit it. Pour out your feelings to God even if they include anger or bitterness. If you feel God has turned away from you, reject the idea as coming from Satan. God loves you! It takes time to adjust to a desert experience but God will help you. What do you have to lose? You will go through the desert anyway. Do you want to go through it alone or with God?

Maybe you've never experienced any of the heavy stuff I've been talking about. Yet you feel depressed. That's okay too. We all go through down periods. When it happens to me, I tend to put on my party-time personality and pretend all is well, but that's wrong. God can't help us unless we admit we need help.

Whether you're facing a major crisis or a minor frustration, God will walk through it with you. Pull good memories from the past, separate the goodness of God from the injustices of life, hang on to your integrity, glorify God, and keep your hope alive. Wherever you are in life's journey, will you pray this prayer with me?

Jesus, you are my example as I learn to deal with suffering in this world. No matter what happens, I will never be called upon to suffer as you suffered. I am grateful you understand what it's like to be human and feel weak and oppressed. Thank you for offering to help carry heavy burdens. Help me give you my sorrows and accept your healing touch. In your precious name I pray. Amen.

***

Sometimes we are without sin and God is silent. At other times God may be silent because of our sin. If God is silent when you pray, ask yourself if it is for any of the following reasons.

- Selfishness (James 4:3)
- Unconfessed sin (Psalm 66:18; John 9:31)
- Pride (Luke 18:11–14)
- Contempt for God's laws (Proverbs 28:9)
- Rejection of God (Proverbs 1:24–28)
- Disobedience (Deuteronomy 1:43–45)
- Living contrary to God's will (Luke 22:42)
- Lack of compassion (Proverbs 21:13)
- Stubbornness (Zechariah 7:9–13)
- Improper request (Jonah 4:3)
- Instability (James 1:6–7)
- Personal ambition (Matthew 20:21)

Rewrite the following prayers in a more appropriate form.

Dear Lord, I can't stand the way my mother treats me. Please help her to become a Christian.

_____

_____

_____

(After wrecking the car while driving under the influence of alcohol) Lord, don't let my dad yell at me for wrecking the car.

_____

_____

_____

Lord, if you'll get me out of this mess, I'll serve you.

_____

_____

_____

Chapter 6
The Maker's Masterpiece

When you look in the mirror, does the face you see wear a smile or a frown? A smile means you like what you see, but a frown spells trouble for your self-esteem. With a healthy outlook on life and help from God you can put a smile on your face and keep it there.

The first step in building positive feelings about yourself is to consider your origin as created by God. Remember, "God saw everything that he had made, and indeed, it was very good" (Genesis 1:31). Rejecting yourself means, in a sense, rejecting God. "O LORD, you are our Father; / we are the clay, / and you are our potter; / we are all the work of your hand" (Isaiah 64:8).

Accept Your Appearance

Some people base their worth solely on personal appearance. They want a different color or texture of hair; they want to be taller, or shorter. It is rare to find someone who is satisfied with his or her looks. The Bible has something to say about how we're made. "Will what is molded say to the one who molds it, 'Why have you made me like this?' " (Romans 9:20).

If you were to watch skilled potters at work, you would wonder how they turn a dry, cracked piece of clay into a beautiful vase. As they began to mix water with clay, you might look at the muddy mess and wish they would quit playing around and get on with making the vase.

Even after the potters twist, turn, beat, and mold the clay, you would not see something that looks like a vase. But then they place the clay on a potter's wheel. They spin the wheel and continue to work the clay by hand. Keeping the clay moist with water, they gently press the vase into shape. When the process is complete, they set the vase aside to dry. "You can't hurry the making of a vase," the potters explain.

The next day the potters go through a similar procedure. Finally, the vase is taken to a kiln and placed in the oven. The door is closed. As the temperature rises, you wonder if the vase will crack in such terrific heat, but the master potters remove it at the right time to paint it, gloss it, and make it a product of fine beauty. You look at the vase and marvel it was ever an ordinary lump of clay.

This is how God will work in your life, too. You were not a mistake when you were created, but God will continue to fashion you according to your destiny if you will cooperate. With God's refiner's wheel and furnace, the rough edges of your life will be smoothed away and your personality will reflect beauty from within. As you yield to the Holy Spirit's control, God's image will be yours. It will show in your life and you can feel good about yourself.

If you don't like the way you look, maybe you can do something about it. Make the most of your positive qualities and minimize anything that detracts from your appearance. For instance, a person who is overweight might overlook the fact that he or she has attractive facial features. Discovering even one personal asset might change an attitude from "I'm hopeless and there's no use trying" to "I'm going to slim down until my body makes my face look even better."

Most overweight people would rather have a slim figure than a hot fudge sundae. Since it takes time to lose weight, though, they often choose the sundae because they can enjoy it now. To postpone pleasure and achieve a long-term goal requires a strong desire as well as discipline.

Jesus asked a man who had been ill for thirty-eight years, "Do you want to be made well?" (John 5:6). The question is a good one to ask yourself if you need to lose weight. If your answer is yes, ask Jesus to help you and then go at it with all the gusto you can muster.

Improving your appearance won't make God love you more, but it may make you feel better about yourself. A more positive self-image will contribute to your overall well-being. Once you do all you can to correct any physical flaws, accept your appearance as a gift from God. If you are not self-conscious about your imperfections, others will notice them less.

Improve Your Performance

Self-esteem often depends upon one's performance. If you bring a *C* in advanced algebra up to a *B*, you usually feel good about yourself. You receive a boost from any accomplishment such as making a team or landing a part in the school play. Make an investment in yourself by trying to improve.

As you strive to do and be your best, you need not compete with others. That leads to frustration and defeat because others will always be better than you in some way—especially if you compare your weak points to their strong points. Find one thing you do well and seek to excel in that area of your life.

When I was a junior in high school I developed a bad case of acne. I'm talking major trauma—the kind that turns off guys and halts your social life. At first I thought, "I'll lick this problem one way or another," but everything I tried failed. If anything, the condition got worse with treatment.

My up-front personality wanted to take a back seat. I wanted no part of being a cheerleader any more because it put me in front of people where I felt everyone was looking at my face. I even heard girls at school whisper about me and make comments almost too painful to repeat.

One night my will to cope copped out. I threw myself across my bed and sobbed. Dad came in to see how he might help.

"What's wrong, Lori?" he asked.

"Dad, you don't know what it's like. I'm ugly. I can't stand myself anymore. I don't want to see people. I just ..." My sobs told the rest of the story.

My father sat quietly on my bed for a few moments as he stroked my hair. "Lori," he said, "I'm really sorry. I know it's tough, but you can overcome this because you're a fighter. You need to forget about your face and start to work on your inner qualities."

"I don't have any inner qualities," I said through stifled sobs.

"Yes you do. Work on your personality or your enthusiastic spirit. You're a positive thinker. Make that work for you now."

I thought maybe Dad was just trying to make me feel better when there was no reason to feel good. Even so, I grasped a faint hope. "Do you really think it will work, Dad?"

"I know it will. Someday the inner qualities you develop will shine through to the outer qualities. You'll see."

I wasn't totally convinced that Dad knew what he was talking about, but I decided to give it a try. I didn't have much to lose and maybe a lot to gain.

The idea came to me that I could focus on loving people. What group of people needed love? I asked myself. I decided people in nursing homes need love and, for a worthy cause, my parents would allow me to use the car! I was itching to make more use of my newly acquired driver's license.

I went to a nearby nursing home and said to the receptionist, "I want to visit a person who gets no visitors."

"You're in luck," she said. "You have the whole nursing home open to you."

Her words broke my heart. Recognizing the hurts of others began to take my mind away from my own pain. The residents listened with interest to my stories. Soon they began to tell me stories from their past. I learned how much they needed someone to just sit and listen to them.

Every Tuesday and Thursday I went to the nursing home. I needed the residents there as much as they needed me. When they told me I was beautiful, I forgot about my face.

One day I visited with a chronically depressed woman named Mrs. Smith. She had been a school teacher and had not adjusted well to her loss of dignity. As I talked with her, she seemed to return to life. Before I left, she said, "Will you do me a favor?"

"If I can."

"When you leave, would you say, 'Good-bye, Mrs. Smith. I …' "
She paused as if to think over her request. "You don't have to
mean it," she said, "but would you just say you love me and you'll
come back and see me?"

I agreed to do as she asked. "Thank you," she said. "I have
nobody else in my life to say those things."

As I turned to leave, Mrs. Smith asked me to repeat my
farewell speech louder in the hall. She wanted the nurses to hear
that someone cared for her.

I did not say the words merely to make her feel better. I said
the words because I meant them. When I left the nursing home
that day, I felt beautiful. I was a queen in that misery-filled nursing home. While I was loving the unlovely, they transformed my
life and changed my negative self-image.

What is your strong point? Choose something you do well and
focus on developing that quality to the max.

If you can't think of any area in which you excel, maybe you
aren't considering enough possibilities. If you don't make the
honor roll, maybe you do well in one particular subject. Are you a
promising athlete? Maybe you're a klutz on the ball field, but you
play a mean piano. Maybe you meet people well and know how to
carry on a good conversation. Perhaps you are a fast, efficient
worker. You might even be a slow worker but accurate with
details. You don't have to be a whiz in your field to begin. Take
even a minor measure of success and build it into a major
achievement. If you still can't think of anything good about yourself, you might want to discuss your feelings with your parents,
your pastor, or a Christian friend.

Be Yourself

Acting is great on the stage, but when you try to be someone
else in real life, you cramp your own style. You do an injustice to
yourself, to God, and to the person you try to imitate.

Do you know that we have the freedom to be ourselves? We

can enjoy whomever God made us to be. Guess what! There is only one Lori Salierno in the universe. That doesn't impress some people, but I'm going to be the best Lori Salierno I can be! I'll do it by being what God expects me to be—myself.

I used to let it get to me when people said something like, "Lori, you're too dramatic! You need to calm down." Or, "Lori, don't talk to everyone you meet." "Lori, why do you have to climb mountains, lift weights, or go hiking, or bike riding? Why can't you do the things other women do?"

Do you know something? I tried to fit the mold some people created for me. It didn't work. I tried to be less dramatic. I tried to be more quiet and reserved. I even tried to cross-stitch. I got totally off center. All of a sudden I felt as if I were in a straitjacket. I wasn't being me and I asked God what to do about it.

When the answer came, I knew it was all right for me to climb mountains or jump from an airplane in a parachute if I so chose. I have the freedom to be myself because that's how God created me.

You don't have to be an uptight, grim-faced Christian who hates yourself! Chill out! Be yourself! As long as you reflect God's glory, you have freedom. If you're the quiet, reserved, intellectual type, don't try to bounce off the walls with me. Let God use your personality as it is. You are unique. If some people don't like the way you are, that's okay. Not everyone can like you, but never allow anyone to make you feel you are less worthy than somebody else.

Forget the Past

Hanging on to your past failures and regrets will hinder a healthy sense of self-esteem. Remember, your past is forgiven if you have received Christ as your Savior. With Paul you can say, "Forgetting what lies behind and straining forward to what lies ahead, I press on toward the goal for the prize" (Philippians 3:13–14).

One day a girl in the Bible study I was teaching announced she had invited a girl named Tonya (not her real name) to attend our meeting.

Some of the other kids protested. "Lori, she's a sleaze! We don't want her here." One of the girls said, "I'm really scared for her to come here." I thought they were overreacting until Tonya came to class.

"Who's the leader of this group?" she asked.

"I am." Somehow my voice lacked a ring of authority.

"Well, what do you teach?"

My confidence returned. "I teach the Bible."

"I'm not so sure I want you to teach it to me," she said.

Tonya overruled everything I tried to do in that session. When she left, the kids gave me the I-told-you-so routine.

"Okay, you guys, let's pray," I said.

The next week a girl I'll call Luann came to class and said, "Hey, you guys, God spoke to me."

"Tell us about it, Luann," I said.

"I was on the bus," she said. "Tonya was throwing spit wads and yelling and cussing and being as ornery as ever. We always got off at the same stop. Just before we got there God said, 'Luann, I want you to tell Tonya that you love her.'"

They got off the bus. Luann wasn't too sure God had a good idea, but she said, "Tonya, I have to tell you something. I love you."

Fire blazed in Tonya's eyes as she said, "Shut up!"

Luann repeated the message from God.

"You say that one more time, and I'll take my fist and I'll hit you in the face!"

"I had a decision to make," Luann said. "I decided to go with what I thought was right. Well, Tonya kept her promise. I went flying! I thought, This is love? I hit the pavement, scraped my face, and tasted blood in my mouth."

"Tonya pointed her finger at me and said, 'That'll teach you never to say that you love me again!'"

With tears in her eyes, Luann looked up at the girl who had

known nothing but abuse and hatred, and said, "Tonya, I love you."

Tonya melted. She knelt beside Luann and began to weep. "Nobody ever loved me like that in my life. How can you do it?"

Luann wiped some of the blood from her face and said, "Tonya, one day a man came to me and said that he loved me. I told him to shut up and go away, but he kept coming back. His name is Jesus. Because he died for me, I can say I love you. He loves you too."

When Tonya came back to the Bible study, she had a different attitude. She allowed Jesus to free her from the garbage of her sordid past. Along with the garbage, she got rid of her hostility toward herself and others.

Obey God

As a Christian, you will have trouble maintaining your self-esteem unless you keep your spiritual experience up-to-date. Actually, your only claim to excellence comes through the Lord. "Let the one who boasts, boast in the Lord" (2 Corinthians 10:17). It is not what you do that deserves acclaim but what God does through you.

If you fail to live up to what you know to be right, feelings of guilt will diminish your sense of self-worth. You cannot continue to violate God's will or neglect your devotional life and still feel God's approval on your life.

On the other hand, obedience will put you in a right relationship with God. As you allow God to create a divine image in you, you can look in your mirror and see a smile because you are the Maker's masterpiece.

Remember the words of the psalmist, "I praise you, for I am fearfully and wonderfully made. / Wonderful are your works; / that I know that very well" (Psalm 139:14).

Here is another prayer to help you give yourself more fully to God.

God, thank you for creating me in your image. Thank you for loving me the way I am. Help me to love and accept myself as you do. Help me to accept myself the way you created me. Help me to enjoy being the person you created me to be. May I make the most of the personality, talents, and gifts you have given me. In the name of Jesus I pray. Amen.

***

Some people recommend shopping to boost self-esteem. Of the following items, which ones would you like to pick up at God's Shopping Mall? Place a check mark (√) beside the items you need the most.

Shopping List
_____ Designer fashions described in Ephesians 6:13–17
_____ Beauty aids described in 1 Peter 3:4

Vitamins as follows:
_____ Vitamin A—Affection (Romans 12:10)
_____ Vitamin A—Abundant life (John 10:10)
_____ Vitamin B—Blessings (Psalm 24:3–5)
_____ Vitamin B—Benevolence (James 2:17)
_____ Vitamin C—Courage (Psalm 31:24)
_____ Vitamin C—Charity (1 Corinthians 13:13)
_____ Vitamin D—Diligence (2 Peter 1:6)
_____ Vitamin D—Determination (Ephesians 6:18)
_____ Vitamin E—Endurance (Matthew 10:22)
_____ Vitamin E—Enthusiasm (Galatians 4:18)
_____ Vitamin K—Kindness (2 Peter 1:7)
_____ Vitamin K—Knowledge (2 Peter 1:5)

Part II

Excellence in Relationships

Chapter 7
Human Sexuality in Holy Spirit Temples

Do you know the difference between a hot dog and a steak? A Volkswagen and a Mercedes Benz? Of course you do, but what makes the difference? A hot dog will fill you up as well as a steak. A Volkswagen will get you to school as well as a Mercedes Benz.

Some products have the same function, but at least two characteristics set a steak and a Mercedes Benz apart from a hot dog and a Volkswagen, respectively. Both are created with a higher standard and both cost more. The standard and the cost determine the quality.

God's standard of living is higher than the standard the world sets. God's standard, clearly stated in the Bible as God's will, is a universal principle that applies to all people no matter where they live or what their culture is like.

God says to Christians, I want to lift you high above mediocrity. I want to exhibit you as an example of my high quality of creativity. If you will pay the price to govern your life by God's standards, you can be that example.

In striking contrast to popular culture, God says, "The body is [not] meant ... for fornication" (1 Corinthians 6:13). What constitutes fornication or sexual immorality? Sexual immorality is any form of sexual activity except that between husband and wife. "Because of cases of sexual immorality, each man should have his own wife, and each woman her own husband" (1 Corinthians 7:2).

When I was in seventh grade a guest speaker came to our

church to talk to the youth. He explained that God intends sex to occur only inside of marriage and not outside of marriage. "The best thing you can give your spouse is your virginity," he said.

After the conference, I went home and wrote a letter. I wrote, "Dear God, Not that anybody would ever want to or anything, but I'm going to be a virgin when I get married. Love, The Big V." I placed the note in my underwear drawer and accepted it as God's nonnegotiable standard for life.

Besides standards, Christians also have deep convictions. Christian convictions are strongly held beliefs based on an individual walk with God. You may believe it is right for you to do something that I couldn't do, and vise versa.

The Corinthian church had a problem with their convictions. New Christians who came out of idol worship did not believe it was right to eat meat that had been offered to idols in religious ceremonies. The more mature Christians knew the idol didn't exist; so for them the ceremony had no effect upon the meat. Quite a controversy developed and Paul was called to arbitrate.

Paul recognized the validity of the argument of the more mature Christians, but he wrote, "If what I eat causes my brother to fall into sin, I will never eat meat again" (1 Corinthians 8:13, NIV). If you seek to be God's example of excellence, you must govern your life with biblical standards and develop Christian convictions that lead you to become all that God designed you to be.

How do you develop Christian convictions? Here's how. Ask yourself questions about any activity or event. Check out music. Movies. Books. Does what you want to do promote anything that goes against God's standard regarding sexuality, alcohol, drugs, or tobacco? Is the language appropriate for a Christian? Does it glorify God? Does it bring you under its control? Will it cause a brother or sister in Christ to stumble? Will it help you mature as a Christian?

When I was in my first year of college I had a running partner. He was kind of cute and I liked him so it made exercising fun. After one of our workouts he said, "Lori, uh how would you like to go out on Saturday?"

I thought, "Wow! A date. Seize this moment." So I said, "Yeah,

I'll go out. That'll be great."

He suggested we eat and see a movie.

Saturday came and we went out to dinner and talked about our running styles and our dreams to be world-class runners. Then we went to a movie.

During the first ten minutes of the movie I began to sweat behind my ears because of what was happening on the screen. I got fidgety as I watched things start coming off of people—things being clothes. When the clothes came off, the people would come together and I got more nervous.

The guy said, "Wow! What do you think?"

"I don't think I like it."

"Keep watching. It gets better." I watched but it didn't get better.

I said, "Lord, what do I do?"

God said, "Lori, if I were sitting next to you in the flesh, what would you do?"

"I'd ask you for a ride home."

"Then you need to leave."

I cleared my throat two or three times and finally the words squeaked out. "I have to go."

"Bathrooms are out back," he said.

"No, I have to leave. I can't watch this movie."

"Why not?"

"Because I'm a Sunday school teacher." We argued and I tried to explain I wouldn't watch the kind of movie I told my students not to watch. Finally, I got up and started toward the door. He stomped out after me.

We were arguing when we got to the foyer. The guy behind the popcorn stand said, "Well, check out the fight tonight."

The guy was fighting mad all the way back to my dorm. Neither of us spoke a word. When we arrived he stopped the car and said, "Please get out. I want you to know, Lori Marvel, I will never take you out on another date. I spent good money on you and you can't handle a mature movie. Now get out!"

I went to my room, threw myself on my bed, and started to cry. I said, "Lord, you know I don't get that many dates. When I do, being a Christian with convictions isn't much fun."

We didn't run together any more. The guy wouldn't even talk to me in the cafeteria. A few months later I was at work when he approached me. "Lori, may I ask you a question?"

"Yeah," I said. I knew he didn't want a date!

"Have you ever been in a locker room after practice with about twenty-five naked men?"

"Now, let me think," I said. "Ummm, no, I don't believe I've been in that situation."

"Let me tell you what it's like." He told me the favorite topic of the guys is young women. He said they discuss their body parts in detail and how much they can get from certain women. "Today your name came up in the locker room," he said.

One of the guys had said, "Hey, has anyone ever dated the Marvel chick?" Everyone got quiet.

The guy who ridiculed my standards and convictions said, "I have. And I want you to know you'll not get anything from her. If you bring up her name again this way, I'll deal with you personally. Lori Marvel is a lady."

Do you know how I felt in that moment? I wanted to grab my standards and convictions and cling to them with every ounce of strength I possessed.

The thirty-ninth chapter of Genesis tells one of my favorite Bible stories. Joseph had been sold to Potiphar, the captain of the temple guard in Egypt. Although he was a slave, Joseph found favor in Potiphar's eyes—so much so that Potiphar put Joseph in charge of his household.

All went well until Mrs. Potiphar arrived. She was what you might call a sleaze. I imagine her wearing her clothes to entice men and knowing how to move her body to attract attention. Well, Mrs. Potiphar noticed Joseph, who was "handsome and good-looking" (Genesis 39:6). Mrs. Potiphar came right to the point and said, "Joseph, go to bed with me." Would you call that forward or what?

Joseph refused her offer and explained his convictions. Mrs. Potiphar didn't understand. Maybe she didn't want to understand. She hounded Joseph with one thing in mind—sex. He did his best to stay away from her.

One day Joseph was the only servant in the house. Maybe Mrs. Potiphar arranged it that way. While Joseph performed his duties, Mrs. Potiphar came up behind him and grabbed his cloak. "Come to bed with me," she demanded.

Fire blazed from Joseph's eyes. With righteous anger he shouted, "No!"

Mrs. Potiphar held tightly to Joseph's cloak while Joseph broke free from her and ran out of the house. "Rape," she screamed and called her servants in as witnesses.

When Potiphar came home, his wife played the role of the innocent victim. "Honey, I was minding my own business when Joseph made sport of me and tried to rape me." She showed her husband the cloak she claimed Joseph had left behind.

Without giving Joseph an opportunity to defend himself, Potiphar sentenced Joseph to prison. What a terrible price to pay for living by his standards and convictions. At that moment Joseph might have felt God had deserted him, but he didn't know the rest of the story. Two years later God honored Joseph. God elevated Joseph to the position of prime minister of Egypt!

I got another date when I was in college. This time, the guy was out of college and had money. Even better, he had a car—and not just an ordinary car. A flashy car. In church one Sunday he came up to me and said, "Lori, want to go out?"

Bells began to ring and music started playing in my head. "Sure I want to go out. That'd be wonderful."

We made a date for Friday night. I went home and called my family together. "I have good news," I said.

"What is it?" Mom asked.

"Got asked on a date."

My brother Bob said, "Oh—what sucker was that?"

"So-and-so."

My other brother Jerry said, "Whoa—the one with the car? He asked you out! What's wrong with his eyeball?"

"Nothing. He just recognizes beauty when he sees it."

Dad said, "Lori, did he actually?"

"Uh-huh," I said with great satisfaction.

My dad got serious. "Now, Lori, you know his father is very influential in our church. He has a high standing in our community. You're pretty privileged to have him ask you out."

"I know. I feel pretty good about it."

Friday night came. The guy drove up in his car and I thought, "Oh, man, let's just feast our eyes on his car." My date got out of the car and started toward the door. Dad said, "Now, Lori, try to be your—uh, not yourself. Okay? Try to be something that's impressive."

"Okay, Dad, I'll try to be a lady."

The guy came in the house and played the part of a perfect gentleman. He said all the right words to Dad and Mom. He patted my little brothers on the head. They said, "Wow, look at his car."

As we got in his flashy car I hoped someone I knew would see me as we drove down the road. We went to a fancy restaurant where all the waiters have white napkins over their arms. I was so used to McDonald's, I didn't know how to handle luxury. We were seated at a window table where we could see barges going down the Columbian River. In the candlelight, with a handsome guy across from me, I felt glamorous.

"Lori," he said.

"Yeah."

"Tell me about some of the goals you have for yourself."

Now that was just about the best question he could ask me. I began to talk about my goals to reach the universe for Jesus Christ. I told him I wanted to do this and that, go here and there, and be influential in the world because that is what God wants us to do. "I am excited," I said.

"That's interesting," he said. He asked me about this and

that—all the right questions. He pushed my buttons like crazy. I thought, He is such a wonderful conversationalist, although I am doing all the talking. I liked being with him.

After dinner we got in his car. He put the key in the ignition, but he didn't start the car. He looked at me for a moment and then said, "Lori, did you have a good time?"

Happiness oozed out of my pores. "Ohhh, I had a wonderful time!"

"So, I showed you a good time."

"Um-hmmm."

His voice was tender. "I've shown you a good time. Now I'd like you to show me a good time."

My happiness began to evaporate. "Didn't you have a good time?"

"Let me put it another way. I paid for your meal. Now you pay me."

"I don't have any money."

"I'm going to put it in terms that you will not have to question. I want a piece of your flesh."

"Dingdong!" I thought, "Buddy, the only flesh you're gonna get is my fist in your face if you don't cut it out." I said, "I'm a godly woman. You don't mess with godly women." Then it dawned on me. "Oh, my goodness," I said. "You don't know about the note in my underwear drawer."

"What about a note in your underwear drawer?"

"Well, it reads like this: 'Dear God, Not that anybody would ever want to or anything, but I'm going to be a virgin when I get married. Love, The Big V.' "

He said, "I don't care about the note in your underwear drawer. All I care about is getting what I want. You aren't going to get home tonight until I get it."

"I'll walk home!"

"You won't walk home because it's too dangerous out there."

"It's more dangerous in here. Take me home—NOW!"

His anger flared all the way home. When I went in the house, my dad asked how everything went. Did I ever have a story to tell him.

The next Sunday the same guy came up to me in church and asked if I wanted to go out on Friday night.

I couldn't believe it. "Are you a sucker for pain or what?"

"No, but I'd like to go out with you again."

I agreed to go out with him on certain conditions. On Sunday afternoon we would meet at McDonald's. He would allow me to talk about Jesus Christ the entire time. "Are you man enough to handle that?" I asked.

"When do we start?"

"Today. Meet me at McDonald's at 3:30."

As we drank a Coke, I started telling him about Jesus. I told him what Christ meant to me. I quoted Scripture.

We met week after week for eight weeks. Finally, he said, "Lori, I don't have what you're talking about."

"Yeah. That's why I'm here with you right now." I wanted him to know God has a different standard for Christians.

Will you accept God's standard regarding sexuality? Anything less than the biblical standard of purity comes from the world. Do you know where the world gets its standard? Straight from hell! The bigger the lie, the better Satan likes it. He will put it in the minds of guys to tell girls, "If you love me, you'll give me what I want." He'll encourage women to come on strong to guys. When Satan sets the standard, wrong seems right. Living together before marriage actually seems like the way to prepare for marriage. Perversion is accepted as an alternate lifestyle. Satan lies and the world believes him.

Don't let it bother you if you're the only virgin around. The best will always be a small group. Why should you want for yourself what the enemy offers? Do you want syphilis, gonorrhea, damaged emotions, pregnancy, abortion, AIDS? They're part of the world's package. Be the one, the only one if necessary, with Christian convictions and God will honor you.

Do you know how God honored me? He gave me Kurt. Kurt doesn't have a lot of money, but he's one good-looking man. Kurt doesn't have a flashy car, but he shares my passion to win the world for Jesus Christ.

Don't violate your body, which Paul described as a temple of the Holy Spirit (1 Corinthians 6:19). Human sexuality is a beautiful gift from God if you govern yourself by God's standards and your convictions.

Sometimes I hear people say, "My body has already been violated for me in rape." If you have been raped or sexually molested, I want you to know God's grace covers you. God does not hold you responsible for that. Through God's grace and perhaps a Christian counselor, you can receive healing and wholeness.

Others say, "It's too late. I've already blown it." Again, that's Satan speaking. God will forgive your past, cleanse you, and lift you to a new standard of holiness. You may have a price to pay for your failure, but that price will only go higher if you continue to follow the ways of the world. Why not allow God to restore you to purity through the cleansing blood of Jesus?

Alexander the Great wasn't a Christian but he was a powerful leader who conquered the Persian empire. He was afraid of nothing and expected his soldiers to be men of courage. When the king held court, cowards received a stiff sentence—often death.

One day a young man about seventeen years old was brought before Alexander. "What is the boy's crime?" the king asked.

The sergeant replied, "Sir, he was fleeing in the face of the enemy and found cringing in a cave."

Alexander's face hardened. He started to speak, but then he noticed innocence in the face of the boy. His countenance softened. "Son, what is your name?" he asked.

Feeling the king's sympathy, the boy sighed in relief and spoke his name. "Alexander."

The king cringed and said, *"What is your name?"*

"Alexander, sir."

Again Alexander the Great asked the boy to repeat his name.

"A-al-exander, sir," the boy stammered.

With indignation mounting, the king stood up, grabbed the boy by his tunic, lifted him off his feet, and slammed him to the ground. "Soldier, change your conduct or change you name."

What is your name? Think about it. What is your name? Dare you take the holy name Christian and live a life without God's standards or your convictions?

***

Pray this prayer: Jesus, look into my heart and reveal to me a standard that is based upon your Word. Point out any convictions that are not high enough. Convict me of anything in my life that violates your design for my sexuality. Forgive me where I have failed. Heal my hurts from the past.

Thank you for your gift of human sexuality. Thank you for the beauty it can bring to life. Help me cherish this gift and apply your standard to my conduct. May I keep my body so pure the Holy Spirit will be pleased to dwell in me. In the precious name of Jesus I pray. Amen.

Now, on the appropriate lines write out personal qualities you have to offer a mate. On the opposite line write the qualities you want to find in a mate.

What I Offer	What I Want

What additional qualities do you wish to add to your own profile? What steps will you take to develop those qualities?

Chapter 8
Playday on the Boss's Time

Whether you go to school or to work, the idea of an eight-hour day may turn you off. If so, why not opt for a playday and collect a payday besides?

"Oh, yeah," you say, "that sounds great, but what about my teacher or boss? They're not going to like it. Besides, how does that fit in with all this stuff you've been teaching about excellence—not to mention honesty?"

Okay, you got me on that one, but stick with me and I'll prove that you can have fun either at school or on the job and still have God's approval upon your life.

Develop the Right Attitude

If you're not enjoying school or work, maybe you need to change your attitude. Work, either at school or on the job, is not something we do just to get by. Work is an opportunity, a privilege, given to us by God. Work provides us with the opportunity to develop virtue, or moral excellence. Virtue, in turn, helps create habits that strengthen character.

When I was in ninth grade, I quit my twelve-dollar-a-month paper route to take a job in a day care for twelve dollars a week—a four hundred percent pay hike. As I collected my twenty-four dollar paycheck every two weeks, I began to feel rich as well as a bit cocky. Going home one day, I came up with what seemed to be a great idea, and so I called a family conference.

"Mom, Dad," I began what I thought to be an unselfish proposal on my part. "I really appreciate the $2.50 I get each week, but I've decided I no longer need an allowance. Since I'm a working woman, I'll give up the $2.50 and you can give it to my brothers. I just wanted to let you know I won't be doing any more chores around the house. My brothers can clean the bathrooms, empty the trash, and perform my duties because they'll be splitting my allowance."

My mom looked at my dad and he looked at me. "Lori," Dad said, "you obviously have not grasped a certain concept in the Marvel home. We are not paying you to do the chores. You do the chores because you're a Marvel and everyone helps with the household chores. Since you no longer need an allowance, we will divide it between your brothers next month, but we are going to increase your work by two chores a day."

"What! I have to do two extra chores and get no money?"

"That's right. I want you to understand that the work of the home will go on. You don't need to get an allowance if that's what you choose, but you will do your part around the house because you belong to this family."

Meeting Obstacles Head-On

You can go to work or school with the right attitude, but even that doesn't guarantee your job will be easy. In fact, it may seem as if you run into more than your share of hurdles. You might have to deal with an unreasonable teacher, boss, or critical co-workers, but you can take heart from the story of Joseph (Genesis 39—45).

Sold into slavery by his brothers, Joseph had no choice but to work for Potiphar. A man of God had to serve a man who did not recognize the existence of God.

Joseph could have had a pity party, but his integrity and hard work eventually earned him the highest position in Potiphar's household. When unjustly accused and thrown into prison, Joseph represented God in such a manner that the guard placed him in charge of the other prisoners. When released from prison,

Joseph worked himself up to second in command of Egypt. He rose from prison to power with God's help and hard work.

No matter where Joseph worked, his superiors could say, "I wish I had more people like Joseph." Can our employers or teachers say that about us? As students or workers, Christians should be the best workers on the job. We should be the ones who come back from lunch early. We should be the ones who support our employers and treat our co-workers with respect. We represent God to the world, and the signature we place on everything we do should match our profession of Christianity.

Meeting the Critics

The story of Nehemiah's leadership in rebuilding the wall of Jerusalem provides some keys for success in any endeavor (Nehemiah 4). First, Nehemiah shows us how to handle our critics. He probably heard remarks like, "What do you think you're doing? You don't know how to build that wall. The way you're going at it, it'll break down if so much as a fox climbs on it."

As Nehemiah pursued the project, he stopped to pray. Do you know the best way to deal with criticism? Turn it over to God and let God handle it. The work that Nehemiah was doing was too important to allow his critics to slow down the process.

When you are trying to do your best for God, either inside or outside the church, you'll meet with opposition. A guy in the shipping department of a small company was hustling to get out tools that customers wanted. "What are you trying to do—cheat us out of our overtime?" a co-worker said. Don't allow anyone to rob you of the joy of work through ridicule.

A sixteenth-century monk named Brother Lawrence spent his entire life in the kitchen of the monastery washing dishes. Brother Lawrence might not have had menial labor in mind when he took his vows to become a monk, but he prayed as he washed dishes, "Lord, be glorified in these clean dishes." He turned the kitchen into a sanctuary of praise, and people who worked with him sensed God's presence in the kitchen.

Fighting Fatigue

When Nehemiah's wall around Jerusalem reached half its height, the strength of the laborers started giving out. A half-finished job can look mighty discouraging. That's when Nehemiah called "time out" for rest and reflection. He grouped the people into families so that they might gain strength and courage from one another.

Halfway through high school or college the tough times ahead may drain you of enthusiasm. Perhaps your job is about to do you in. Call time out. Seek counsel from someone who has made it through school or someone who understands your job—perhaps your teacher or your boss. Draw from the wisdom and experience of someone who knows what you are going through. As you pray, allow God to refresh your spirit, and nothing can keep you down.

Your extracurricular activities may be more responsible for your fatigue than your job or your studies. Sometimes it's necessary to give up the tennis match or the lead in the school play to devote more time to the work God is calling you to do.

Focusing beyond the Rubble

As the wall of Jerusalem went up, rubbish piled up. The people were discouraged and all they could see was rubbish. What did Nehemiah do? Nehemiah said, "Remember the LORD, who is great and awesome" (4:14).

When we look at our work and see nothing but rubbish, we must refocus our eyes on God. No honorable work is too lowly, no task is too insignificant to merit our signature of excellence. A job well done becomes a praise offering to God.

In my first two summers in college I cleaned toilets to earn money to help pay my way through school. That's not my favorite job, but payday came around every week and that was good. My dad liked that part too. The longer I was on the job, however, the better I got at cleaning toilets. And you know something? The better I got at cleaning toilets, the better I liked my job.

By my third summer I was getting pretty good or something because I got a promotion. No more grubby uniforms for me. No more grimy toilets either. I got to wear my best clothes, sit behind a big desk in the courthouse, and answer the phone and take messages. I even had a title and a nameplate to prove it: Receptionist. Notice the Capital *R*.

When the phone would ring, I would pick it us and say, "Good morning, may I help you?" I used my most professional voice, but the gentleman on the other end still asked for Mr. Brown.

"I'm sorry, Mr. Brown isn't in. May I take a message?"

"Tell him to give me a call." I took down the man's name and number and wondered what he wanted with Mr. Brown. My job would be more exciting if I could get in on some of the action, I thought.

One day I was at work and a guy about eighteen years old walked in. My counterpart from previous summers—the toilet cleaner. He pushed a maintenance cart stocked with cleaners, brushes, mops, and rags. His head was down, his shoulders drooped, and he shuffled along as he pushed the cart.

He disappeared into the bathroom and when he came out a few minutes later, his head was still down and his shoulders drooped.

"Hi, sir," I said, "My name is Lori. What's yours?"

Without looking up, he mumbled, "Dexter," and walked out.

Two days later, he came back and I said, "Hi, Dexter, how are you?"

I can't be sure, but I think I caught a slight flicker of movement from his Adam's apple and I may have heard a faint sound like "uh." He went into the bathroom again to clean.

On his way out, I called to him. "Hey, Dexter, before you leave, may I tell you something about yourself?"

That caught his attention and he stopped the cart, but he didn't look up. At least I could hear his one word even if I did detect a hint of scorn in his voice. "What?"

"You don't like your job," I said.

Dexter raised his head to half-mast. A spark began to penetrate the lackluster expression of his eyes. "Ma'am, I clean toilets for a living. Get a clue. I hate my job!"

I said, "You know what? I cleaned toilets for two solid summers eight hours a day to get through school. Not only have I cleaned toilets, but I'm the best toilet cleaner this side of the Mississippi."

Dexter came up to my desk and looked me straight in the eye. "So what!"

"So—the next time you clean this bathroom and this toilet, I'm going to grade you."

"How do you grade a toilet?"

I explained the grading system used when I was in school: *A*, *B*, *C*, or *D*. I decided to leave out the *F*. I didn't think Dexter's self-image could handle total failure.

Shaking his head, Dexter said, "You are weird!" As he walked out, I noticed his head go down and his shoulders droop.

The next week Dexter walked in pushing his cart, came up to my desk, looked around and said, "Like, are you going to grade my toilet?"

I looked up from my work to give him my full attention. "Yeah."

After about fifteen minutes in the bathroom, Dexter came out and said, "Don't tell the secretary what you're doing."

"I won't," I promised.

I went in the bathroom, lifted up the toilet lid and said, "Dexter, what goes here?"

He said, "Well, I didn't think you would look at that."

"This is gross." Picking up a piece of toilet tissue, I said, "What's this?"

"The tiniest piece of toilet paper I ever saw."

I pointed to splashes of water all over the place and announced, "Dexter you get a *C* for today.

"*C*!" he exclaimed.

"Yes, Dexter, a *C*! Remember, I'm an expert toilet cleaner."

When Dexter walked in the next time, he stood a little

straighter and held his head a little higher. He walked by my desk and said, "You're grading my toilet today. Is that right?"

He stayed in the bathroom for twenty-five minutes and came out sweating. He was almost panting as he said, "I'm ready for you to grade my can!"

I went into the rest room, lifted up the lid, and nodded my head. "Major improvement, Dexter." Scanning the floor with my eyes I observed, "No paper—oops, Dexter, what's that on the spigot?"

Dexter squinted his eyes for better vision. "Two tiny water spots," he said.

"Okay, you get a *B*."

"What?" he squealed.

"*B*, Dexter. It's *B* work. You'll get an *A* when you do *A* work."

I was on the phone when Dexter came in the next time, but he came right up to my desk and shoved a toilet brush in my face. As soon as I hung up the phone, he said, "I'm going to get an *A* today or else!"

"You'll get an *A* when you do *A* work!" I said.

He went in the bathroom and I could hear the scrub, scrub, scrubbing and the flush, flush, flushing. Forty-five minutes later he came up to my desk and said, "Get in there!"

The bathroom was so clean I could have eaten my supper on the floor! I beamed at him and said, "Dexter, you get an *A*+!"

He got excited and yelled so loud I thought the secretary would come in to see what I was doing with that guy.

Dexter wanted me to meet his buddies. At break time I met eight or nine guys in the basement. One guy said, "I hear Dexter got a major *A* on his toilet today."

"Yeah. Actually *A*+!"

"So—is Dexter like good or what?"

With my most dramatic flair I said, "Dexter is premier in toilet cleaning."

Dexter stood two inches taller with his shoulders squared and his head held high. "Feeling good!" he said.

Some of the guys wanted me to grade their work too. One trimmed hedges and another washed windows. I don't know much about trimming hedges and I don't do windows, but I realized that those guys needed someone to help them see the value in their work.

"I don't think I could get away with running all over the courthouse to check up on you guys, but you know what? You can grade your own work. Better yet, grade each other's work. Be tough on yourselves. Demand excellence, and you can stand as tall and proud as Dexter here."

I cooked up a spur-of-the-moment party. Actually, we just chopped up some Snickers bars and passed around the pieces.

"So—why are we partying?" one guy asked.

"Because you're valuable," I said. "What you guys do in this place is important. You are just as important as the judges and lawyers. And I want you to know that you are special because God designed you that way."

Dexter learned that his attitude can make the difference between drudgery and delight in work. I hoped the other guys caught the same vision.

Fighting Failure

A sense of failure can cheat you out of having fun with work, but one thing is certain. If you're ever going to accomplish anything, you're going to experience failure! What? Failure? When I get my degree, I'm still gonna fail? Yeah.

After rising to become a noted novelist, critic, and dramatist, George Bernard Shaw said, "When I was a young man I observed that nine out of ten things I did were failures. I didn't want to be a failure, so I did ten times more work."[3]

Failure is part of the game called work. When you fail you feel let down—ready to quit. In the fourth chapter of Nehemiah, the people said, "We cannot rebuild the wall" (v 10, NIV), but their mission was accomplished in chapter six. "The wall was completed ... in fifty-two days" (v 15, NIV). Can you imagine what kind of a party they threw?

Do you know at what point your frustrating, irritating, disappointing work will turn into a playday? When you overcome poor attitudes and fear of failure. And the harder you work to win, the greater will be your pleasure when you achieve success.

Before Michelangelo became a famous sculptor, he worked as a gardener for an Italian duke. As he tended the garden one day, his eyes reveled in the beauty all around him until he focused on the flower boxes. Somehow the plain boxes seemed out of place in the splendor of the setting. Michelangelo's mind went to work. He pictured an intricate design on the flower box. His vision was so clear that he got his chisel and began to chip away the stone to create the image that formed in his mind.

Meanwhile, the duke decided to go for a walk in his garden. An unfamiliar sound caught his attention and irritated him because the noise disturbed the serenity of the early morning. He walked toward the sound and soon came face to face with Michelangelo. "What are you doing?" he asked.

"I'm chiseling a design on this flower box."

"Why?"

"Sir, I want the flower boxes to match the grandeur of your garden," Michelangelo replied.

The duke protested in a strong voice. "Flower boxes don't merit such intricate work," he said.

Michelangelo looked the duke in the eyes. With intense emotion that surged through his soul, he responded, "But, sir, my spirit does!"

Does your spirit demand a signature of excellence on everything you do? Is your work a praise offering to God? You may work on something as simple as a flower box today, but if you do your best, tomorrow may bring success beyond your highest expectations. The master of the faithful servant said, "You have been trustworthy in a few things, I will put you in charge of many things; enter into the joy of your master" (Matthew 25:21).

To get the most from your work, ignore your critics, focus on God, fight failure, and never complain. Whether you empty trash or design computers, whether you're a blue-collar worker or a white-collar worker, consider your work as a gift from God and use it to develop virtue—a character trait that brands you as a Christian.

Please pray the following prayer.

God, I want to pause and allow my mind to dwell on the excellence of your divine nature. With the psalmist I say, "Praise him for his mighty acts: praise him according to his excellent greatness" (Psalm 150:2, KJV).

Lord, send your Spirit to ignite me with a fresh, new vision regarding my work. Thank you for the opportunity to carve my signature on flower boxes to match the grandeur of your universe and your character. Help me to stamp the name of Jesus Christ on everything I do. Amen.

***

Read and reflect upon these questions.

How can you play the following games on your job, as you do chores around home, or even while doing your homework?

Do you like to play tennis or volleyball when points count up during your turn to serve? On the job, you have even greater chances to score because your turn to serve never ends. As you rate your service record, you'll be cheated out of some of the fun you're entitled to if you can't applaud your progress. If serving isn't your idea of fun, check out Matthew 20:26.

Maybe you'd rather play baseball. Shouldn't it be as much fun to increase production on the job as it is to increase your batting average? It can be. It's up to you and your willingness to play ball. If you think Proverbs 22:29 is shooting high, would you settle for a pay raise or a better grade?

When counting your mistakes, make it a game of golf. Keeping the score below par is a game for everyone to play. Why not try for a birdie? Then better it. Decide how long you need to go without a mistake for a hole-in-one. A week? A month? Proverbs 18:9 describes people who fail to play golf on the job.

Chapter 9

Fighting Forces of Evil

Shortly after I moved to Washington, some of my new friends in sixth grade were talking about participating in a seance.

"What's a seance?" I asked. I had never heard of a seance in Louisiana.

"Come and stay the night at my house on Friday and we'll show you," one girl said. "My mom does great seances."

The other girls showed so much excitement I accepted the invitation.

On Friday night, all went well until they turned out the lights. Everyone started acting strangely, and the whole place seemed a bit spooky. They lit a candle and began to chant. As they chanted, I began to get edgy. Because the mother took part, I tried not to panic.

When they stopped the chants the party got worse. The mother looked at me with narrowed eyes and spoke in an eerie tone of voice. "Now, Lori, the time has come. The spirit will now live with you."

All eyes were fixed on me. I wanted to run from the room, but I stammered, "Uh, uh—what kind of spirit?"

"Look around you," the woman said. "The girls in your class have had the evil spirit to live in their homes. Now, because you have moved in, the evil spirit must live in your home." I looked around and did not want the kind of spirit that showed in the girls' faces.

"But we already have a spirit living in our home," I said.

"Every spirit has a name," she said. "What is your spirit's name?"

I hoped my words could be heard above the thumping of my heart. "His name is Holy Spirit," I said, "and there is no room for any other spirit."

The other girls began to laugh. "Lori's taking it all in. She really believes this." They were right. I was so scared I was out of my wits.

The mother walked toward me. She opened her eyes so wide I thought they might pop out. She put her hands on my head and said, "Now the evil spirit is within you. You must take it home. It will live in the Marvel home." A shiver went down my spine and I wanted to scream.

They turned the lights back on and everyone returned to normal except me. I spent a sleepless night.

The next day I rushed home and said, "Mom, Dad, come in the bedroom quick."

We went in the bedroom and I collapsed on the bed.

"Lori, what is it?" Dad said.

"Dad, we've got company."

"Well, where are they?"

I could almost feel the color draining from my face. "Right here in this room with us."

"Lori, what are you talking about?" Dad said.

"Last night I received an evil spirit, and he now lives in the Marvel home."

My dad's face took on an expression I had never before seen. "Where did you get this evil spirit?"

I told them everything that had happened.

My parents didn't laugh. They didn't say, "Oh, Lori, that's a bunch of garbage." My dad said, "Lori, look me in the eye." My eyes met my dad's eyes as he said, "This is nothing to play around with because it is real! It is real!"

Recognize the Unseen World

People can go to different extremes regarding Satan. Some deny the devil exists. Others become preoccupied with the works of Satan.

We don't want to overdo it, but we need to be aware of the unseen world. The daily newspapers often point out the results of worshiping Satan with animal and human sacrifices. If the secular press recognizes the reality of the unseen world, how much more should Christians be alert to what the devil is up to.

Do you realize the unseen world actually is more real than the physical world we see? That's an awesome thought. Someday the physical world we know will cease to exist, but the unseen world will continue forever.

While we're in the physical world, the unseen world will give us more trouble spiritually than the seen world.

"Our struggle is not against enemies of blood and flesh, but against the rulers, against the authorities, against the cosmic powers of this present darkness, against the spiritual forces of evil in the heavenly places" (Ephesians 6:12). Paul was not talking about Star Wars; this is a real battle against a real being. Satan is not just a vague idea about evil. Satan is a real being with a mind to plan strategies and an army to help him carry out his objectives.

Just as there is an unseen world representing Satan, there is spiritual world representing God. A good example comes from the Old Testament. During a war, the king of Aram set out to capture Elisha, one of God's prophets in Israel. One morning Elisha's servant woke up to find the camp surrounded by an enemy army. The horses and chariots left no way to escape. Full of fear, the servant went to Elisha and asked, "What shall we do?"

The prophet answered, "Do not be afraid, for there are more with us than there are with them" (2 Kings 6:16).

Seeing no one around, the servant probably thought that Elisha had flipped out for sure. After Elisha prayed, "The LORD opened the eyes of the servant, and he saw; the mountain was full of horses and chariots of fire all around Elisha" (2 Kings 6:17).

The forces of good and evil are in a battle and we're caught in the cross fire. Before we judge our chances of winning, however, we need to know how strong our enemy is. Satan is powerful, but there is a limit to his power. If we serve God, Satan is powerful in our lives only to the degree we allow him to be.

Prepare for Battle

"Therefore take up the whole armor of God, so that you may be able to... stand firm" (Ephesians 6:13). God's armor provides us with both offensive and defensive weapons. With the weapons God provides, we can penetrate the power of darkness and minimize the power of evil.

Basically, our spiritual weapons fall into four categories. Our first weapon is—simply—the power of the name of Jesus. "At the name of Jesus / every knee should bend, / in heaven and on earth and under the earth, / and every tongue should confess / that Jesus Christ is Lord" (Philippians 2:10–11).

The name of Jesus has greater power than anything else on earth. When we pray in the name of Jesus, we connect with his power. When we speak in his name, we connect with his power. We can impact both the unseen and the physical world through the power in Jesus' name.

When I started out in the ministry, I worked as a counselor. One day another counselor, Jill, and I took some kids to the city to witness about Christ. After everyone understood his or her job, Jill and I found a quiet spot and sat down on the grass.

I was just beginning to relax when Jill poked me. "Hey, Lori, look over there." I looked and I cringed.

The guy I saw was really weird! His hair stuck out in every direction, all kinds of junk hung from his ears, and big chains circled his neck. If the shackles around his wrists had been connected, he would never have been able to break free. His jeans had writing all over them and he must have used mascara to draw big black circles under his eyes.

I said, "Jill, he must have gotten up this morning and said, 'How can I make myself look the most weird today?' That's ridiculous. Absolutely ridiculous! What a jerky thing to do!"

As I expressed my opinion of the guy, Jill interrupted. "Hey, Lori, want to go tell him about Jesus?"

"Not on your life I don't! That guy's too far gone to rescue." I knew that wasn't true, but that was how I felt.

Jill got up and reached her hand to me. "Come on, Lori. I'll talk and you pray."

"I'll pray from here."

"No, no, come with me," Jill said as she pulled on my hand. "You don't have to say a word. You just pray, and I'll share the gospel."

"Oh, Jill, why do you have to be so Christian?" I said as I allowed her to pull me to my feet.

We walked across the grass and sat down next to that stinky guy. He looked at us and said, "What do you two want?"

"Tell him, Jill," I said. "Tell him what we want."

Jill sat so still I thought she had gone into a trance or something. "Great!" I thought. "Jill?" I said.

She didn't answer. Finally, I cleared my throat and spoke. "Well, sir, we were sitting over there noticing your attire, and we wanted to kind of know where you're coming from. We just wanted to meet with you." Talk, Jill, talk! I wanted to scream.

The guy stared at me with wild eyes and said, "Lady, I'll tell you where I'm coming from. I am a follower of Satan! I live for his kingdom, and he reigns within me."

By that time I was feeling more evangelistic fervor. "Is that right? Well, sir, you're going to be really excited when I tell you I'm a bona fide, signified, born-again Christian! I follow Jesus Christ!"

The guy looked like he had just been struck by lightning. "Lady, don't say that name around me."

"Name? What name?" I tried to pretend I didn't understand, but he didn't respond. "Oh, you mean the name of Jesus Christ?"

Between clenched teeth he said, "I said don't say that name around me!"

"Why does that name bother you so much, sir?"

"I don't know, but I hate it!"

I looked straight into his evil eyes. "I'll tell you why you hate it! You hate the name of Jesus because that is the name that brings your lord, Satan, to his knees! You and your god are powerless under that name!"

By his expression, I could tell the guy was a true follower of Satan. "Get out of my face!" he said.

Suddenly, Jill's ability to speak returned. "Sir, you don't have to wear those chains around your neck any more," she said. "You don't have to wear those shackles on your wrists. Jesus can free you from them. You can be free! You don't have to dress the way you do. You can even wipe off those circles around your eyes."

Fire burned from his eyes. "Get out of my face—both of you!" he shouted.

We stood up and started to walk away. Jill turned around and said, "In the name of Jesus Christ, God loves you."

What power we have in the name of Jesus! Even the sound of his name causes Satan to tremble. When we pray in the name of Jesus, we not only move God, we defeat the enemy as well. "The Son of God was revealed for this purpose, to destroy the works of the devil" (1 John 3:8). When Jesus comes on the scene, Satan must flee.

One of the best ways to silence the forces of evil is with Scripture. Hebrews 4:12 describes the Word of God as "sharper than any two-edged sword." How's that for an effective weapon?

After his baptism, Jesus retreated to the desert to fast and pray that God would guide him in his ministry. As soon as Satan gained Christ's attention, he came on strong. Satan sought to mess up God's plan. But Jesus answered every temptation with Scripture. Satan hates Scripture except when he can twist the meaning to make himself look good.

The power available to us through the Holy Spirit provides us with an effective tool to attack the enemy. "You will receive power when the Holy Spirit has come upon you; and you will be my witnesses ... to the ends of the earth" (Acts 1:8).

We receive the Holy Spirit as we unconditionally give ourselves to God and ask for the Spirit to fill us. In order to mature in faith, we may need to repeat the request from time to time.

For example, suppose you go away to college and have a roommate for the first time in your life. You soon discover the two of you are opposites. Little things annoy you. Before long, you're ready to scream every time your roommate walks in the room. One day you lose your cool and say things you soon regret. At that point you seek help from the Holy Spirit to adjust to the give-and-take requirement of a close relationship. Every time you face a challenge you can't handle, you will need to pull power from the Holy Spirit.

We can also war against Satan as we share the gospel message. In fact, we might call the gospel our spiritual atomic bomb. Someday God will end Satan's regime. In the meantime, the devil's stronghold on earth diminishes every time an unbeliever responds to the gospel.

Some situations call for a combination of these weapons. When I lived in Indianapolis I took a group of students to Haiti to get a better understanding of missions. During one church service a man crashed into the building screaming, waving his arms, cursing, and spitting. Two American pastors went over to the man and said, "In the name of Jesus Christ we rebuke you." The pastors began to quote Scripture while the man continued this demonic behavior. Finally, after forty-five minutes, the man went limp. At that point one of the pastors said, "Would you like to receive the Lord Jesus as your personal Lord and Savior?"

The man said, "For so long I've had another spirit living in me. I'd like to receive the Lord."

During the next service, this man sat next to me as a brother in Christ. The power of the gospel broke the devil's strongholds in his life.

Take Action

I was quite impressed by that experience in Haiti. I'd never seen anything like that take place before. When I got home I thought, I'm going to try that. I had a particular guy in mind who needed to be free from the devil's influence. Not long before, he had sat in my office and said, "I can't believe God is who he says he is." He was really messed up and needed the Lord, but Satan didn't want to give him up.

I began to pray. I prayed warfare because I saw in Haiti how much work it took to defeat the enemy. My arms were waving and I was going strong when Kurt came home and thought I had lost it. I just kept on praying that God would deliver the guy.

The next time the guy came in to see me, he had changed his life. "Lori, something melted my heart," he said. "I don't know about my unbelief; I don't know about my hatred. All I know is this: I need Jesus." That man got on his knees and sobbed as he confessed his sins to God.

God's power works to defeat the stronghold of Satan! But victory comes at a price. It won't happen from a postscript to "Now I lay me down to sleep." Breaking Satan's bonds calls for action— the kind of action that says we're dead serious! The disciples asked Jesus why they had failed to cast out an evil spirit from a boy. Jesus replied, "This kind can come out only through prayer" (Mark 9:29).

When we go to a ball game we let everyone know that we're out to win. The cheerleaders shout, "A-C-T-I-O-N, action, action!" and we follow along with all the gusto that's within us. We cheer for a victorious outcome of a ball game, but what are we doing about a world that is going to hell?

Will you take up the fight that goes on every day in the unseen world? Will you ally yourself on God's side against the devil? The stakes are high. "The god of this world has blinded the minds of the unbelievers" (2 Corinthians 4:4). Millions of people blinded by Satan can receive their sight only through the power of the gospel and your prayers.

What can you do? Keep your experience strong in Jesus Christ. Exercise the power of prayer in the name of Jesus. Soak your mind with Scripture—read, meditate, and memorize God's Word. Seek the Holy Spirit's power for victory over failures. Gain a position of confidence—not a position of cockiness in yourself—but a position of confidence in Christ.

Move beyond your own spiritual battles to fight the power of darkness in those around you. At school, pray prayer arrows at the heads of your friends and your enemies. In the cafeteria, ask God to feed the souls of those who serve you or eat with you. Take the joy of the Lord with you into a shopping mall and watch your presence make a difference in those around you. Always be aware of people who are in the grips of the enemy. Ask God to show you how to penetrate darkness with the light of Christ.

If you assume spiritual warfare as a lifestyle, you will change the unseen world. With your spiritual weapons, you can go forth as a soldier of the cross and come through trials more than a conqueror.

God, I'm so thankful that you are the Lord of the universe. You have already won the war in the battle that is now taking place in the unseen world. Thank you for the victory that is mine through Jesus Christ. Help me to use my weapons well. In the powerful name of Jesus I pray. Amen.

***

Referring to Ephesians 6:14–18, list below the spiritual weapons for fighting forces of evil. Then with a marker highlight the weapons you now use, such as the "helmet of salvation." Choose a weapon you wish to strengthen and highlight in a different color. What action will you take to receive greater benefit from this weapon?

Spiritual Weapons in Ephesians 6:14–18

_____

_____

_____

_____

_____

_____

_____

_____

_____

_____

Chapter 10
Spiritual Energy Supplement

God is brilliant! When designing human beings, God thought of everything. Knowing we would need all the help we could get, God established the church as both a channel and a source of spiritual energy.

Some people think it isn't necessary to attend church to be a Christian. "If I've accepted Jesus as my Savior, that's all that's necessary," they say. Well, that might be true if they're stranded on an island. Under unusual circumstances, the Holy Spirit will make up for the lack of a support system.

Isolation from other Christians is not God's plan. "Let us not give up meeting together, as some are in the habit of doing, but let us encourage one another" (Hebrews 10:25, NIV). Jesus built the church for a reason.

What do we get from church that we need? As we participate in worship with other Christians we are inspired. As we sing praises together and unite our hearts in prayer we are strengthened. As we hear God's Word preached we hide it in our hearts to keep us from sin. Powerful messages and good illustrations help us better apply God's Word to our lives.

During the three weeks I spent in Russia, I began to realize what a precious privilege it is to worship together as Christians. In the Baltic state of Estonia, where I shared the gospel in the public schools, I attended church and was impressed by the many expressions of joy on the faces of Christians as they worshiped.

For many years, Russians were deprived of the privilege of worshiping together as a community. I met one woman who didn't understand English, and I didn't understand Russian, but we were kindred spirits. I hugged her and said, "I just want you to know I love you. You're my sister in the Lord." As she put her arms around me, she cried so hard her body shook. Tears of joy streamed down her face because she was able to freely worship the Lord with others. I gained enormous appreciation for my church back home.

Not all religious groups use the Bible as their rule for faith and life, even when they claim to. A congregation that encourages a personal relationship with God is on the right track. Still you have to be careful where to worship and serve. Some cults teach that you can reach God through your personal resources alone.

The key to reaching God, however, is Jesus Christ. Does the congregation you attend teach Jesus is the only Son of God? Does it teach that salvation comes through the death and resurrection of Jesus Christ? Are you are saved by grace through faith (Ephesians 2:8)? Does it teach the necessity of a personal relationship with Jesus as Savior and Lord? These questions require positive answers. The Bible instructs us to "Test the spirits to see whether they are from God; for many false prophets have gone out into the world. By this you know the Spirit of God: every spirit that confesses Jesus Christ has come in the flesh is from God, and every spirit that does not confess Jesus is not from God. And this is the spirit of the antichrist" (1 John 4:1–3).

As you read the Bible and pray, the Holy Spirit will guide you to a congregation that will minister to your needs as well as provide you the opportunity to minister to the needs of others.

Join a Small Group

Even if you attend church once, twice, or three times a week, something may still be lacking from your spiritual diet. The structure of most worship services fosters communion with God, but communion with other Christians may be missing. Too often, in our relationships at church, we do not reveal our true feelings.

People may say, "Hello, how are you doing?"

"Doing great."

"Good. Good to see you. See you next week."

As these casual greetings occur in the church, the people behind the masks may have something quite different on their minds. One of my mentors told me I should visualize every person I meet as someone with a burden. I usually find that to be true.

So where do you go when you need counsel, advice, or support? You might go to a psychologist or psychiatrist if you have enough money and are willing to spend it for that purpose. If you do need professional help, you would be wise to seek a Christian counselor. They are more sensitive to spiritual matters and do not base their advice on standards of the world.

Your may not need professional help, however. You may just need to bounce ideas back and forth with a Christian friend. It's good to talk about what's going on in your life with someone who cares. At one time or another you'll want to talk about friendships, dating, the possibility of marriage, relating to family members, schoolwork, or your dreams for the future.

The smaller the group, the more inclined people are to bare their emotions. No one wants the whole world to know his or her private affairs. Some groups are designed for the primary purpose of providing individual support.

Congregations today have begun to provide opportunities for people in similar situations to meet together in small groups with an emphasis of supporting one another with prayer and concern. The traditional Sunday school class separates us by age and sometimes interests. In the past, we have emphasized learning rather than relationships. Fortunately, this is changing.

Take the Initiative

Suppose you join a small group and no one opens up to you. You could change groups, of course. On the other hand, it might be to your advantage as well as to others to make the first move.

A woman once walked into a Sunday school class where the

mood had always been formal. Although it was her first visit, she sat down and burst into tears. Encouraged by the teacher, she poured out her story of the hurts that haunted her. As people reached out to her, they began to reveal their own emotions. Feelings of closeness developed that class members had not previously experienced. From that one session, times of personal sharing became routine in the class. One woman took the initiative.

You may not want to create such a dramatic scene. A simple question might break the ice. Asking questions may encourage others to open up and share their personal experiences. As trust builds, inhibitions will disappear.

Perhaps you can find one person who will serve as your spiritual friend. Because a wicked woman had vowed to kill Elijah, he took refuge under a tree and wanted to give up. Keep in mind this was a prophet of God who had prayed fire down from heaven. But his moment of triumph had passed, and Elijah was discouraged. What did God do? First God provided for Elijah's physical needs with sleep and food. Then God sent Elisha to encourage Elijah. From that point on, Elijah had a kindred spirit in Elisha— someone to relieve his loneliness and share his pain.

When David was running from Saul, God sent Jonathan to him. Jonathan warned David of danger and put his own life on the line to spare David.

If a prophet of God and a king anointed by God needed encouragement, will you not need someone to support you when you are down? I like the way one young woman expressed her expectations of the church. "If I move away from God, I hope someone will love me enough to bring me back," she said. The Bible makes a similar statement: "Woe to one who is alone and falls and does not have another to help" (Ecclesiastes 4:10).

Find a person or a group composed of people who have a close walk with God. The ideal person or group will help you feel comfortable and yet challenge you to grow. When you can admit to another person you are struggling, help is on the way. You become accountable to a brother or sister who says, "I'm praying for you. Hang in there."

If you do not have a support group to love you, ask God to

direct you to one. If you do not have a soul mate to keep you accountable—someone to pick you up if you fall—pray that God will bring you together with the right person.

Respect a Confidence

Secrets of the heart make colorful topics for conversation. Most of us are interested in the private lives of others. Some people in the church possess an unhealthy desire to know what goes on with everyone else. To be accepted and popular, you might be tempted to reveal information you have received in confidence.

To violate someone's trust is a serious offense whether or not your intent is malicious. "A gossip goes about telling secrets, / but one who is trustworthy in spirit keeps a confidence" (Proverbs 11:13). Betraying someone's confidence marks you a gossip. Don't even ask other people to pray about the private concern of another person that was shared in confidence. Bridle your tongue and do your own praying.

While careless words hurt the person whose secret is exposed, they also can damage the one who talks. Even the people who enjoy gossip will have reservations about the person who reveals confidential information. What kind of treatment can an informant expect when he or she wants to keep a personal matter quiet? Anyone tempted to tell a private matter that belongs to another person should consider the consequences.

Minister to Others

Do you know why God ministers to you through the church? God meets your need through the church so you can minister to others. It's a great system, really. God relates with the church and the church members relate with one another. Christians who have lived through a crisis often say, "I couldn't have made it without my church family."

"I'm the weak one," you might say. "I don't have anything to offer to anyone else." Oh, yes you do! Do you know that you can lift up someone who is down simply by being available? You don't have to have all the answers. You don't need to come up with a brilliant solution to the problem. You may need to do nothing but listen.

Many people are quick to give advice. You may know people like this. You begin to describe your problem. Before you speak the first sentence, they say, "Trust God," which sounds easy but isn't. Instead of receiving encouragement from that kind of person, you become more frustrated.

Chained in a cold, dark dungeon with death awaiting him, Paul, the apostle, longed for fellowship with other saints. Alone, with the Lord and his memories to comfort him, Paul wrote his second letter to Timothy. In that letter Paul said that everyone in Asia had turned away from him, including two disciples whom he mentioned by name. Paul did not dwell on his disappointment, but can you imagine how he must have felt? For thirty years he had given himself in ministry, and those who worked with him had deserted him!

Instead of grieving over what he had lost, Paul rejoiced in a fond memory. "May the Lord grant mercy to the household of Onesiphorus, because he often refreshed me and was not ashamed of my chain" (2 Timothy 1:16).

Onesiphorus refreshed Paul, but who was Onesiphorus? Did you read about him in your Bible storybook? Probably not. Onesiphorus is mentioned no place else in the Bible except in 2 Timothy 4. Onesiphorus did not go on a missionary journey. He did not establish a church. Onesiphorus was an ordinary person—maybe even a behind-the-scenes person. Yet he refreshed Paul, the great apostle in the faith. How would you like to have that on your résumé?

Actually, Onesiphorus did more than make himself available to Paul. If you continue reading, you learn Onesiphorus made a special effort to minister to Paul. "When he [Onesiphorus] arrived in Rome, he eagerly searched for me and found me" (2 Timothy 1:17), Paul wrote.

He didn't give up when some of the Christians in Rome said, "No, we don't know where to find Paul."

How long do you suppose Onesiphorus searched for Paul? When others were ashamed to be associated with Paul because of his chains, Onesiphorus intentionally determined to find him, comfort him and, if necessary, share Paul's shame.

What do you suppose happened when Onesiphorus found Paul? He didn't tell Paul to trust God because Paul was already doing that. He didn't promise Paul he would soon be released from prison because Paul was on death row. Perhaps they hugged; then he allowed Paul to talk. Surely Paul needed to unburden his soul. Simply by listening, Onesiphorus took a part of Paul's burden upon himself. Communication flowed from Onesiphorus to Paul without words because they were kindred spirits.

Abandon Yourself in Love

Conditions are more conducive to carrying out Christ's command to love one another within a small group. It is difficult to develop strong ties with people you don't know well. When Christians go through a crisis together, or share a spiritual experience, a spiritual bond forms between them.

Luke recorded the story of a sinful woman who went all out to demonstrate her love for Jesus. The drama took place in a Pharisee's home, where Jesus had been invited for dinner. According to custom, the guests reclined at the table. When a rabbi was present, outsiders were free to come and go in the courtyard where the meal was served.

In spite of the raised eyebrows and disapproving glances, the wicked woman entered the courtyard and stood at the feet of Jesus. His purity in contrast to her depravity caused her to weep. In the presence of Jesus, feelings of remorse prompted her to do something for him. But what could a sinful woman do for the Son of God?

Her eyes focused on Jesus' grimy feet. Where were the host's manners? Because the roads were dusty and shoes were merely abbreviated sandals, a host normally rinsed a guest's feet with cool water. The host's neglect provided the woman with her opportunity. She allowed her tears to fall onto the feet of Jesus. Then she lovingly wiped his feet with her hair.

The gesture still did not satisfy the woman. What else could she do? Like other women of her day, she wore a small bottle of perfume around her neck. Quite possibly this represented the only luxury in her life. She could have dabbed a drop of perfume on Christ's head but she did not feel worthy to anoint his head. Instead, she poured the entire contents on his feet (Luke 7:36–39).

What a way to go! Don't you just love her style? She didn't care who was watching or what anyone thought. She totally abandoned herself to express her love for Jesus. As she breathed in the fragrance, she absorbed not only the beauty of the perfume but also the beauty of Jesus into her life.

The story of this woman reminds me of an experience I had in Haiti. One day our group decided to go swimming in a river. To get back to the mission station we had to climb a small hill. By the time we got to the top, our feet and ankles were covered with mud. The Haitian pastor met us with a pitcher of water and a basin. "I want to wash your feet," he said.

The water lasted for the washing of only four feet. Then the pastor ran down to the river, collected more water, and washed the feet of two more persons. By the time he got to me, he was knee high in mud. "Lori, may I wash your feet?" he said.

I looked at his feet and wanted to trade places with him. "May I wash yours?" I asked.

"No, it's me to you," he said. "What washes my feet is knowing we're part of the same family. We serve one another, do we not?"

Indeed, all Christians are part of the family of God. We were designed to serve and encourage one another. Do you have someone in your life who will support you when you are up and when you are down? Can you bare your emotions to someone who will listen, offer encouragement, and keep a confidence? Will someone keep you accountable if you begin to neglect your spiritual disciplines? If you do not have a support group or a soul mate, ask God to give you one. God did not create you to walk the Christian life alone. Let's pray.

Jesus, thank you for establishing the church. It is a place where I can receive inspiration and where I can minister to others. I love you and I love your church. May I find in it the support I need for my spiritual survival. In your name I pray. Amen.

***

Who is your role model in the Christian life? Might you enlist that person to be your spiritual friend to help you get back on track if you stumble? (Note: Inaccessible persons can still be mentors through their writing or speaking.)

If you are not part of a small group where prayer concerns are exchanged, how can you find such a group? Who might be in your small group? Might you contact them and ask them about forming a small group to promote spiritual growth?

My role model(s) in the Christian life

_____

_____

_____

Persons who might be in my small group are

_____

_____

_____

_____

_____

_____

_____

_____

_____

_____

Part III

Serving with Excellence

Chapter 11
Your Unique Ministry

Do you know God has work to do that may not get done if you don't do it? If such heavy responsibility scares you, it need not. You may not need to preach a sermon or go to the mission field. To have a unique ministry, you simply need to allow God to help you fulfill your unique potential.

You see, God designed the church so that the members are dependent upon God and upon one another. We need God and God needs us. Without us, God may not choose to act. Without God, we cannot hope to accomplish anything that will last. Christian ministry is done through human hands but not by human hands. It requires an alliance between the divine and the human. "Take courage, all you people of the land, says the LORD; work, for I am with you, says the LORD of hosts" (Haggai 2:4).

God's Call

Christians sometimes downplay the importance of answering God's call to ministry. They say, "I know Jesus said, 'Go into all the world and proclaim the good news to the whole creation' [Mark 16:15], but that doesn't have anything to do with me. That's just for preachers."

It is true that preachers have a unique function to fulfill, but ministry involves more than preaching—much more. Jesus said, "The kingdom of heaven is like a landowner who went out early in the morning to hire laborers for his vineyard" (Matthew 20:1).

Ministry consists of any work that is necessary to keep God's vineyard running smoothly. The one who functions in a support role in the church stands as an equal beside the preacher or the teacher in ministry.

In the twelfth chapter of 1 Corinthians Paul compared the various members of the human body with the various gifts in the spiritual body of Christ. Every part is necessary for the welfare of the body and the welfare of the church. It doesn't matter whether you're an up-front person or a behind-the-scenes person. You can participate in ministry. When you recognize your responsibility to work for the Lord, the question becomes, How do I find my place in God's work?

Your talents and personality will help you determine where you best fit. When you give your life to God, God will actually develop a divine plan for your life around your interests, abilities, and personality. The fact that you are different from every other person on earth gives God fresh material to work with.

Do you realize God can use your past experiences and even your failures in ministry? Suppose you play basketball and your friend missed a basket and lost the ball game. Fans jeer as he heads for the locker room. You, on the other hand, meet him with words of encouragement. "I feel like a failure," he says. You pull an experience from your past to ease his pain. "That's how I felt when I failed algebra. My parents didn't understand. They thought I goofed off, but I didn't. I tried. I just couldn't make it." Remember, when you give your life to God, the Holy Spirit will equip and strengthen you for ministry.

God's Vision

When you get serious about ministry for the Lord, you need a vision. "It shall be night to you, without vision" (Micah 3:6). A vision represents something that hasn't yet happened. It's something you foresee in the future as taking place for God. In ministry, your vision becomes your goal and you pursue it with passion.

Don't be afraid to dream big. The bigger your dream, the greater your potential to make a worthwhile contribution to God.

My pastor once made a statement that captured my attention. I wrote it down and refer to it often. "If your dream is small enough for you to handle, it isn't big enough for God." Wow! Doesn't that tingle you right down to your toes?

If you want to start a Bible study, it's okay to believe it might grow to include fifty kids. Maybe God wants to develop your musical ability into a ministry. Go for it! Whatever your personality, whatever your talents, God has a special place where you can serve. There are as many ways to do ministry as there are people.

If you don't have a vision, look for a human need and meet it. That is how God brings vision about. You won't accomplish anything big all at once. Neither does an artist complete a masterpiece with two or three strokes of the brush. Many brush strokes hardly show, but every dinky dab of paint contributes to the beauty of the finished picture.

As you work toward making your goal, there will be times when you feel like throwing up your hands and saying, "I can't do it!" Actually, that's a positive sign because it forces you to recognize your human limitations. Tell God you're stuck and you need help. Scripture promises "To him who by the power at work within us is able to accomplish abundantly far more than we can ask or imagine, to him be glory in the church" (Ephesians 3:20–21). Praise God, your vision is a mighty force that can be energized through the power of Jesus Christ working within you!

Criticism can dim your vision. "Your idea won't work." "It's never been done that way." "I don't understand your line of reasoning." Take an in-depth look at what your critics say. Might they be right? Are there two sides to the issue? Can you acknowledge another point of view without compromising your own position? Learn what you can from your critics but do not allow them to destroy your vision for the Lord. Ask God to heal any hurt and free your mind so you can continue with your work.

God's Power

If your vision is to be backed by divine power, you need to develop three characteristics.

First, you must hate sin. God hates sin. You hate what sin does to people but you love the people. You shudder to think that those who remain in sin will spend eternity separated from God. You get fired up because people are going to hell, and you vow to do something about it!

The second key to a power-packed vision is knowledge of the gospel message. You know all have sinned and need a Savior. You also believe Jesus Christ is the only way to God. You know people must act on their convictions to accept God's guarantee of forgiveness. But you must continue to grow in the grace and knowledge of God's Word.

Sink your teeth into the gospel message and make it the guiding force of your ministry. Focus on the importance of receiving Christ as Savior. "This is the testimony: God gave us eternal life, and this life is in his Son. Whoever has the Son has life; whoever does not have the Son of God does not have life" (1 John 5:11–12). It doesn't matter how good people are or how much religion they have. If they don't have the Son of God, they are lost. That should put urgency into your ministry.

The third trait that marks you as a person of vision is your love for humanity. You will love people of a different race or people who disagree with you. You will love the person who received the award that you wanted or the person who dates the girl or guy you had your eye on. At school, at work, or at home, you will look for hurting people and try to meet that need.

Develop a Strategy: Meet a Need

No matter how potentially powerful your vision, a strategy is required to take it from a dream to reality. At some point, you need to take your vision from your mind and assimilate it into your lifestyle.

The same Jesus who said to go into all the world to preach the gospel also said, "Whoever wishes to become great among you must be your servant" (Mark 10:43). In the church we talk a lot about service. Sometimes we need to stop talking and start serving. That's how Mother Teresa's ministry started. She discovered a dying man on the street, picked him up, and carried him to a hospital that had no place for him. "Lord, how can I help this man die with dignity?" she asked. Her world-renowned ministry evolved from that one experience of meeting a need.

I read Mother Teresa's story with fascination. The desire to participate in what she was doing overwhelmed me. I wrote to ask her if I could bring a group of students to share in her work.

Finally, an answer came to the church office. I made sure everyone in the office knew about the letter.

"Read the letter," someone said.

I began to read, "Thank you very much for your kind letter and offer to come and share the joy of loving by serving our people. You will be most welcome to come. The joy of loving is the joy of sharing and giving until it hurts. Keep the joy of loving Jesus in your heart and share this joy with all you meet."

As I examined the short letter, I noticed she had used the word *joy* five times. What a wonderful way to describe her sacrificial ministry! What would be misery to many people was joy to this woman whose vision had become her life. I anticipated a life-changing experience.

Eleven people and I went to India for two weeks. We worked with the dying; we worked with the children; we worked with the lepers. When the time came for us to leave, however, we had missed the privilege of meeting Mother Teresa because she was in Armenia helping people there.

When we got to the airport in Calcutta we discovered our plane would be four hours late. The airport was crowded. Our group somehow huddled into a circle and started playing games. I paced back and forth, feeling somewhat bored. Excitement replaced my boredom when I heard someone say, "Mother Teresa is coming in the airport." I went to tell my group I was going to meet Mother Teresa, but they didn't believe me. So I went off to prove them wrong.

When I found two nuns, I said, "Is Mother Teresa coming to this airport?"

"Yes," one of them said, "but she cannot be bothered."

"Please, please just let me greet her."

111

"Try to get past those two armed guards."

Two men with guns strapped across their shoulders guarded the entrance to the terminal. I approached them and told them I wanted to go past their barricade to meet Mother Teresa. They allowed me to pass.

The first person to walk through the entrance was a small, four-foot-eleven, wrinkled nun. She looked at me and beckoned me with her hand. I walked up to her and said, "Mother Teresa, you're such a dear lady of God." I took her face in my hands and kissed her on the cheek. "I desperately love you," I said.

In a gentle voice she said, "Do I know you?"

I could feel my heart thumping as I said, "Oh, yes. You wrote me a letter and invited me to come to India. I brought eleven people with me and we've worked in all your homes."

Her eyes reflected the tenderness in her voice. "Let me ask you this, did you enjoy the work?"

"Yes, I did."

She paused, but I could tell that something serious was on her mind. "Let me ask you something else. Did you give until it hurt?"

"I think." I wasn't sure whether my answer represented a statement or a question.

A sweet smile formed on Mother Teresa's face. "What can I do for you?" she asked.

"Oh, the people I brought with me would be absolutely delighted if you would come and greet them."

"Take my arm. Take me to them."

I took hold of that saintly arm. As we approached our group, I said, "I'm bringing her to you."

Excitement mounted as Mother Teresa greeted each person. Everyone wanted to touch her and get her autograph. She asked the group the same questions she had asked me. I took the questions home with me and continue to ask myself on a regular basis, Do I give until it hurts?

Develop a Strategy: Share and Live the Gospel

When I was in high school, my dad often took me with him on hospital calls. One day we visited a woman my dad did not know well. During their conversation, Dad said, "Have you ever accepted Jesus as your Lord and Savior?"

"No, I have never done that," she said.

"May I share the gospel with you?" Dad asked.

"Well—," she hesitated. "Sure." What else could she say with IVs sticking out both arms?

Dad shared the gospel in a very sincere, simple manner. I got excited and started praying, "God, come down hard on her. Get her, Lord, get her!"

When Dad finished, he said, "Would you like to accept Jesus as your Savior?"

"No, I wouldn't!"

The audacity! I thought. She refused a message from the Lord. Dad prayed with her and we left.

In the elevator I said, "Dad, why didn't you just pull out those IVs and tell her she's not going to get them back into her arms until she becomes a Christian?"

Dad looked at me with a stern expression on his face. "Lori, you don't do it that way!" he said. "You don't shove it, cram it, or force it. You share it and you live it!"

The time may come in your ministry when you present the gospel and someone will respond. That may happen the first time or the tenth time around. That's when you need to be prepared to tell someone how to receive Jesus as Savior. That's where you need a thorough knowledge of God's Word.

Develop a Strategy: Evangelize

I believe all Christians are called to evangelism. I sometimes find that my one-on-one witness has a greater effect than my sermons. One time, while I was completing a homework assignment in an airport, a woman walked in wearing tight velvet pants, a black velvet jacket, and black shoes with chrome bands around them. She was definitely her own person; maybe a little hostile, a little rebellious, but unique. I was so intrigued I began to pray God would make the gospel real to her through somebody. As my prayer arrows struck her, she looked at me. I looked down at my book but continued to pray for her.

On the airplane the engines roared to a start and the flight attendant was about to close the door when our last passenger boarded. Guess who it was? The woman in black velvet came to my row and took the middle seat beside me. I thought, "Lord, maybe I'm the one to make the gospel real to her."

After she settled in with her ghetto blaster and a bunch of roses, she looked at my open book. "What's that?" she asked, referring to my Hebrew textbook. I explained I was doing homework.

"You know I'm going to school too," she said.

"You are?" I hoped my interest would encourage her to talk.

"Yeah, to get my GED. I'm going to get my diploma, get a job, and I'm going to get my life together."

"Is your life not together?" I wondered, Where will this lead, Lord?

"No. I was twelve years old the first time I got drunk. At fourteen I tried my first joint. I dropped out of school at sixteen. I got pregnant, had a baby, and gave it up for adoption. My life's a mess and I need to get it together."

I sensed a strong message from God: "Lori, now, now!"

"How have you decided to get your life together?" I asked.

"I don't know. What do you think?"

Wow! What an opening! That was all the encouragement I needed. I began to share the gospel. "Do you know that you can have a personal relationship with Jesus? Through him God will forgive you, cleanse you, make you whole, and give you a purpose in life."

Tears came in her eyes. "I want God," she said. By the time we finished talking, I believed she had enough knowledge to guide her to a salvation experience.

The next day she called me at home. "What you said on the plane really made a difference in my life," she said.

In your daily routine, you will come in contact with people who may never have the opportunity to hear a sermon unless you can bring them into the church. Your friends at school, your teachers, the people you work with—all are good candidates to hear the gospel message.

"They won't listen," you say. "I don't want to pressure anyone into making a decision." God's not calling you to bring people to a decision about their salvation. Only God can do that. Our responsibility is simply to share the gospel and show people how to live the Christian life. God will do the rest.

Develop a Strategy: Give One Hundred Percent

As a young man, D. L. Moody sat in church and heard the preacher say, "The world has yet to see the person who has surrendered to Jesus Christ one hundred percent." In the moment that D. L. Moody heard that statement, he said in his heart, "Lord, I will be that person." Thousands of people came to know Jesus through his ministry because he surrendered himself completely to the Lord.

Will you surrender yourself one hundred percent to the Lord? What is your dream? What is your vision of ministry? With your whole life ahead of you, you can afford to dream big. I challenge you to take the proverb I learned from my pastor and make it yours. Put it in personal terms: "If my dream is small enough for me to handle, it isn't big enough for God." Keep that in mind as you choose your career or your life's mate. Where can you best serve God? Who can help you most in your ministry? Plan every aspect of your life in anticipation of hearing the words, "Well done, good and trustworthy slave" (Matthew 25:21).

***

115

God, when I think of your mighty works, I feel insignificant. Yet you have called me to be a person of vision and a humble servant. You have called me to evangelize. Mold my vision, Lord, according to your design. Work through me with divine power to accomplish your purpose. Help me make the greatest contribution possible to your kingdom. In Jesus' name I pray. Amen.

If you have only short blocks of time to devote to ministry, that may be enough. Jesus asked the disciples to watch with him for one hour, but they failed. In the following situations, identify where you can participate and become a one-hour disciple. Can you think of other situations in which you can serve?

_____ Spend an hour tutoring a child.

_____ Bake a batch of brownies for a working mother.

_____ Send cards or letters to missionaries or to someone who is sick or sad.

_____ Do something unexpected for a parent.

_____ Spend an hour listening to someone with a problem and end your time together with prayer.

_____ Entertain a child who acts up for lack of attention.

_____ Write to a government official about a matter that affects the moral or spiritual values of the country.

_____ Do something unexpected for your parents.

_____ Come up with a new idea of your own.

Chapter 12
Money-Backed Testimony

When we look at life from a Christian perspective, sooner or later we must deal with the subject of money. Ouch! We often get edgy when someone wants to invade what we consider to be private territory. What business does anyone have telling us what to do with our money?

Actually, the Bible has quite a lot to say about money. It talks about people rich and poor.

The rich young ruler turned away from following Jesus because he did not want to give up his wealth. Watching the young man's reaction, Jesus said, "How hard it will be for those who have wealth to enter the kingdom of God!" (Mark 10:23). Wow! How much money can we have before God kicks us out of the kingdom? Does God adjust that figure for inflation?

Wait a minute, though. What about Abraham, Job, Zacchaeus, or Joseph of Arimathea? They were rich and found favor with God. Besides, God seemed to take a fancy to riches. God's blueprint for building the tabernacle called for gold thirty-nine times, along with other expensive materials. If God despises wealth like sin, surely costly materials would have been excluded from the place of worship.

In Mark 10:24 Jesus repeated, "Children, how hard it is to enter the kingdom of God!" Some manuscripts include the phrase, "How hard it is for those who trust in riches to enter the kingdom of God!" This interpretation is confirmed by other passages such as, "If riches increase, do not set your heart on them" (Psalm 62:10).

The very nature of riches fosters a fake sense of security. While knowing where the next meal will come from is comforting, the feeling that wealth can supply every need is deceptive and blasphemous. Trusting in riches eliminates dependence upon God.

A simple exercise will deepen your understanding of this truth. First, read Philippians 4:19. It says, "My God will fully satisfy every need of yours according to his riches in glory in Christ Jesus." Who will meet your needs? The answer is obvious. Now take a dime and place it over the word "God." How does this change your thinking? Can you see how easy it is to allow money to come between you and God?

Money Problems

Spiritual problems related to money come primarily in two forms. First, some people get money in an immoral way. It is our responsibility to make sure we acquire our money through legitimate means. If we work for a living, we give our employer a day's work for a day's pay. If we're in business, we don't cut corners to gain a profit. We don't cheat people to get ahead.

Some people earn their money in a legitimate way, but they are greedy. For them money is not a means to an end, it is an end in itself. If making money is our primary aim, we are motivated by greed. "The lover of money will not be satisfied with money; nor the lover of wealth, with gain" (Ecclesiastes 5:10).

Actually, the love-of-money sin can be committed by anyone regardless of his or her bank-account balance. Like any other sin, greed can be present in the heart whether or not the desire is ever realized.

The second problem centers around what we do with money. How do we make wise choices? Consider everything we own belongs to God. Indeed, all things do come from God. Scripture says "Remember the LORD your God, for it is he who gives you power to get wealth" (Deuteronomy 8:18). As God's stewards, we seek to spend our resources according to God's guidelines.

What are those guidelines? The Law in the Old Testament declares a tithe (ten percent) of our income belongs to God. When the people didn't pay their tithe, God asked, "Will anyone rob God? Yet you are robbing me!" (Malachi 3:8). Wow! What an accusation! Their guilt? They failed to tithe.

The New Testament takes a slightly different approach. "Now about the collection for God's people: Do what I told the Galatian churches to do. On the first day of every week, each one of you should set aside a sum of money in keeping with [personal] income, saving it up, so that when I come no collections will have to be made" (1 Corinthians 16:1–2, NIV). The amount is open, but Jesus set a higher standard than required by Law in matters of morality and human relationships. Would he lower the standard with regard to money? Instead of making tithing a legal requirement, Jesus calls us to give as an act of worship that grows out of love, devotion, and gratitude for God.

Patterns of Giving

In their habits of giving, people usually fall into four basic categories. The first category consists of *nongivers*. They feel no responsibility to give to God through the local congregation. One woman visited a new congregation and passed up the collection plate. After the service she said, "I feel so good when I come to church. Some people give a lot of money, but they don't go to worship. I think it's so much better to go."

Some people become deeply involved in the church, but they won't give. They may enjoy a Bible study or even teach. They may sing in the choir or lead a social group, but their money is theirs.

We must welcome people into worship even if they don't give money. They may benefit from their attendance, but they will miss out on much of God's joy if they withhold their money. Giving is part of God's design for abundant life. Striving for spiritual excellence requires a money-backed profession of faith.

The second category of people might be called *token givers*. They know they should give so they put a dollar or two into the collection plate to ease their conscience. They fear that if they don't give something, God might strike them down. They try to buy God, but they don't want to put themselves out. Such people learn to live with a guilt complex.

According to 2 Corinthians 9:6–7, "The one who sows sparingly will also reap sparingly, and the one who sows bountifully will also reap bountifully. Each of you must give as you have made up your mind, not reluctantly or under compulsion, for God loves a cheerful giver."

Another group of people are *sporadic tithers*. They hear a powerful sermon on tithing and say, "I'll tithe! I'll be that ten percenter! Gotcha! I'm right there with you!"

For a few weeks they give faithfully, but before long they start to hold back. Maybe they don't like the way the church is run. They get mad at the pastor or other church leaders. "Until they start doing things my way," they say, "they can get along without my money." A personal, financial struggle may cause others to quit giving. They say, "I want to tithe, but I can't afford it."

Jesus told a parable to illustrate the sporadic tither (Matthew 13:5–6). Seeds that fell on rocky ground sprang up, but because there was no moisture, they withered. Jesus compared this seed to those who receive God's Word with joy but have no roots. They believe for a while but in times of temptation fall away.

The last group of givers are the *faithful tithers*—people who assume responsibility to carry on the work of the Lord. These people commit their incomes along with themselves to God. They don't need pats on the back. They don't need to read a notice in the newsletter: "Mr. and Mrs. Steward gave a thousand dollars last week." When bad times come and bills get heavy, they still tithe because their income is committed to God.

Sometimes new Christians start out as nongivers and become faithful tithers. I'm thinking of one person in particular—a person who has a special place in my heart. I'll always remember Fred Hall who came to all my ball games when I was in junior high school.

When Fred became a Christian, he knew nothing about the Bible. Looking back, Fred wonders how he could have been so ignorant. He says he learned something new in every sermon—many things he didn't want to learn because they called him to live a more accountable lifestyle. Fred wasn't happy about all the changes he needed to make in his life. Still, he didn't want to lose the peace and joy he felt when the Lord came into his life. So he began to change.

One of Fred's biggest battles started when he heard a sermon on tithing. "Boy, I tell you," he said, "I didn't think that was any-body else's business. If I wanted to tithe, that was my business." But his reluctance to tithe kept haunting him. He tried arguing with his wife, but she wouldn't argue. She wanted him to work it out with God.

As the struggle continued, Fred finally tired of fighting God's gentle Spirit and said, "I'm going to give it a try." After he had tithed for a while, God blessed Fred with a better job. His salary nearly doubled, but he didn't increase his tithe. "I thought the extra money would come in handy somewhere else," he reasoned.

One day, on the way home from work, Fred wrecked his car, turning it upside down. As he crawled out of the bent metal and broken glass, Fred didn't check to see if he was hurt. The first thought that came to his mind was, You didn't pay your tithe. He brushed the thought aside and told himself he was crazy to think that way.

For the next few days Fred jumped on his bicycle and pedaled off to work. One evening, during heavy traffic, Fred changed lanes to make better time. Just as he pulled up beside a truck, the guy driving the vehicle decided he wanted to shoot ahead of traffic. When the driver sped up, Fred and his bike went under the truck.

When it was all over, Fred jumped up, not thinking about bro-ken bones or any other possible consequences. In a booming voice, he seemed to hear God say, "You didn't pay your tithe!"

"All right, Lord, I will!" Fred said. "I will."

"I tell you, God got my attention right there," Fred says.

Dedication and Discipline

You can match your pattern of giving with God's will as you dedicate yourself and all you own to God. That means your pay-check belongs to God, but you will be the steward over it. If that seems like an awesome responsibility, you're right. Your gift to God now represents an attitude of love rather than a sense of obligation.

Good stewardship begins with dedication, but you also need discipline to carry out your intentions. For example, the latest designer label outfit catches your eye in the mall. "Wow! I gotta have that," you say. You count your money. If you splurge, you'll have to shortchange your tithe. Maybe I could make it up next time, you think. No, God comes first, your conscience protests. Discipline takes over and you leave the mall empty-handed.

Since you may not make big bucks at this point in life, you may assume you'll tithe in the future. You think you'll start tithing when your career gets going or when you get married. "Besides," you reason, "what can God do with the little bit I could give?"

Are you in for a surprise! Only on one occasion did Jesus commend anyone for giving. Do you know what that person gave? Two very small coins worth only a fraction of a penny. Jesus commended the generosity of the poor widow because "she out of her poverty has put in everything she had, all she had to live on" (Mark 12:44).

In his autobiography *Up from Slavery*, Booker T. Washington told about raising funds to found Tuskegee Institute.[4] The gift that meant the most to Washington came from an aged black woman. "I'm ignorant and I'm poor," she said. "Most of my life has been spent in slavery, but I believe in what you are doing." From behind her back, the woman brought out six eggs. "I want to help the Institute," she said. "Will you take my eggs?" Washington realized hers was the most valuable gift he had ever received because she gave out of her poverty.

In writing about the saints in the Macedonian churches, Paul said, "During a severe ordeal of affliction, their abundant joy and their extreme poverty have overflowed in a wealth of generosity on their part. For, as I can testify, they voluntarily gave according to their means, and even beyond their means" (2 Corinthians 8:2–3). What a testimony! They gave even beyond their ability. Do you know your checkbook can make a stronger statement about your relationship with God than what you say? Money talks about what is in your heart.

Divine Dividends

Before some people will commit to anything, they want to know, "What's in it for me?" God answers that question by saying, "Bring the full tithe into the storehouse, so that there may be food in my house, and thus put me to the test, says the LORD of hosts; see if I will not open the windows of heaven for you and pour down for you an overflowing blessing" (Malachi 3:10).

Does this mean that you'll prosper if you're faithful in giving to God? Maybe. Maybe not. You might double your salary or you might lose your job. Wow! What about God's promise of blessings? Jesus said, "One's life does not consist in the abundance of possessions" (Luke 12:15). Not all blessings are materialistic in nature.

How much is it worth to you to be in the center of God's will? Would you exchange the joy and peace that accompany obedience for any amount of money? You can be rich spiritually even if you are poor in the wealth of the world.

Suppose God allows you to strike it rich. What will you do with your wealth? Concerning those who are rich, Paul wrote, "They are to do good, to be rich in good works, generous, and ready to share" (1 Timothy 6:18). If God gives you wealth, it is so you can give to others and back to God.

A Personal Challenge

What is your present pattern of giving? Are you a *nongiver,* a *token giver,* a *sporadic tither,* or a *faithful tither*? If you are less than a faithful tither, is that where you want to be in your Christian experience?

I challenge you to see God as the owner of all your resources and yourself as the steward of all your possessions. When you earn money, will you take ten percent from the top and give it to God? Will you give God an offering beyond that? When you plan your budget, will you figure that God's portion is sacred—set apart, untouchable? Will you bring your offering to God as an act of worship?

Through dedication and discipline, you can gain God's approval of the way you handle your money. Begin with this prayer.

God, I recognize your lordship over all creation and over my possessions in particular. Thank you for allowing me to prosper. Thank you for the privilege of promoting your kingdom through giving back to you a portion of what you already have given me. Help me to give of myself as well as of my resources, so my offerings may be acceptable in your sight. In Jesus' name I pray. Amen.

***

Write out your present practice of giving. Identify what kind of giver you are.

_____

_____

_____

What claim does God have on the money you keep? How can you demonstrate that claim?

_____

_____

_____

How does your budget need to be revised to receive maximum spiritual value from the way you handle your finances?

_____

_____

Chapter 13
The Long-Distance Christian

In my senior year in college I took a required sociology class. I had missed taking it my first year and somehow had neglected to schedule it. I figured the course would be a breeze and I just wanted to get it out of the way and graduate.

After our first exam, the professor charted the grades on the chalkboard from the highest to the lowest grade. When he listed the lowest score, I thought, Wow! What poor student got that grade? Well, the professor passed out the papers and guess who got the lowest grade? Yeah, I did. One of my friends said, "Lori, what did you get?"

"Uh, I really don't want to share it."

Someone said, "She probably got the highest grade." I didn't comment on that, but someone else said, "No, I did."

From that point on I didn't have a good day. I had an evening class, so Kurt came to take me out for dinner before my class.

When Kurt picked me up I was steaming mad. "Kurt, do you know what? I got the lowest grade in my sociology class! I'm the only senior with a bunch of first-year students!"

Yes, I said that even though I love first-year students. I continued my tirade. "You know what? I am quitting. If that's how I'm treated, I am quitting! I am withdrawing from this school and it doesn't matter to me if I graduate or not. I quit!"

Kurt let me wind down before he spoke. "So, I'm married to a quitter, huh? Am I destined to spend the rest of my life with a quitter? My wife can't handle a low grade. She is a quitter. She is one term away from her degree, but she's a quitter. I'm married to a quitter. How do you like that?"

Kurt always knows how to help me see the light. I got as fired up about finishing college as I was about quitting. I said, "If you think I'm going to quit because of one low grade, you've got another think coming! I'm going back there and I'm gonna do it!"

On the day I graduated, I didn't remember that humiliating experience. My sense of victory canceled all other feelings.

Don't Quit

The key to successful living is endurance. You need endurance in school, on the job, and in your Christian life—particularly in your Christian life. Jesus said, "The one who endures to the end will be saved" (Matthew 10:22). When you're humiliated, don't give up. If someone ignores you at church, don't quit. If you feel God has deserted you, remember the Lord's promise to be ever present with you. If you disappoint yourself and God, do not despair. Keep trying until you turn your failure into success.

Do you know what I want on my tombstone? When I die, I hope my tombstone reads, "We couldn't keep her down!"

Knock me down and I'm up! Knock me down again and I'm back up. I just want to keep coming back up no matter how hard or how often I'm knocked down. I want to endure to the end.

When he was a boy, Winston Churchill was kicked out of a private boys' school he attended. Years later, the same school called Winston Churchill to return as chapel speaker. Do you know what he did? He stood before those boys, squared his shoulders, and said in a voice ringing with authority, "Never give in, never give in, never, never, never give up ..."[5] With his message delivered, Winston Churchill sat down. He had given the boys his key to success.

A More Excellent Way

What will give you the power to endure to the end?

Sometimes it will be your faith. Sometimes your prayer life will see you through. Other Christians or joy will carry you at times, discipline and determination at other times. And, of course, God's Word as recorded in the Bible is forever true and a source of strength for your Christian life. Yet there is more.

At the end of 1 Corinthians 12 Paul wrote, "I will show you a still more excellent way." Paul continued by writing the familiar chapter on love, 1 Corinthians 13, often read at weddings. If you follow Paul's advice about showing love you will never go wrong. It can strengthen a marriage or provide the endurance to hang on to God when life gets tough.

Some people seem to be born with a loving disposition. Others must work at it. Whether love comes naturally for us or not, it is impossible to love as Paul tells us to love in our own strength. We need God's love. When we feel unable to love someone, we can go to God and say, "Lord, I don't have it in me to love. Give me your love." As we allow God to develop divine love in us, we will miraculously be transformed and able to touch others with that love.

When I lived in Edmonds, Washington, I taught a junior high Bible study class. I had read about a particularly effective teaching method and I decided to try it with my students. The first time we met I said, "Okay, turn to 1 John 4:7–21. Put a bookmark there because we're going to stay right there until we begin to practice what it says."

Then we began to talk about love. Week after week after week we talked about love. "No matter what anyone does to you, respond in love," I repeated. Still, I saw no demonstration of divine love in their lives.

One day when we opened our Bibles a guy I'll call Ernie said, "Well, I want everyone to know that this is the last time we're going to discuss 1 John 4."

Ernie was heavyset and fun to be around; yet he could be serious when he wanted to be. I just loved him.

"Why is that, Ernie?" I asked.

"Because I lived it."

That was reason enough for major excitement. "What happened?" I asked.

"Well, I went to one of my classes and the teacher was late. One of the big football players came in and he said, 'Hey, jelly belly.' I was looking at my book but I knew he was talking to me. Without looking up, I said, 'What?' "

"The guy said, 'Put that belly out so we can hit the target.' He took a piece of paper and wadded it up and threw it. Pretty soon all of the kids started throwing paper to see if they could hit my belly. I sat at my desk and felt humiliated, but I kept looking at my book and they started talking about my fat belly, my fat lips, and my fat body."

"Ernie, I'm really sorry," I said. "I wish that hadn't happened because I want you to know I think you're beautiful."

At the interruption, Ernie raised his hand. "Lori, be quiet. My story's not over. The teacher walked in and everyone got quiet, but I had little wads of paper all around my desk. The teacher said, 'Pop quiz. I want everyone to get out a piece of paper.' "

"The big football player said in a smart-aleck way, 'I don't have any paper. I used it all for a good cause.' "

"The teacher said, 'I want someone to give this boy a piece of paper.' "

Ernie paused for a moment and then turned up the volume of his voice. "I got a word from God. I opened my three-ring binder and took out a piece of paper. I stood up, walked down the aisle and across the front of that room and went to that boy and said, 'Here's your piece of paper.' My class got quiet. Then I walked back to my seat and sat down."

All of us listened in silence as Ernie continued. "After class, I was so embarrassed that I wanted all the kids to leave before I got up to go. I stared at my book. The kids left but I could see two legs standing by me. The guy said, 'Hey, jell, why'd you do it?' "

"I said, 'Do what?' "

" 'Why did you give me a piece of paper when I made fun of you?' "

I couldn't wait to hear Ernie's answer. "Lori," he said, "I did exactly what you've been telling us to do all these weeks. With all the God I had within my big body, I said, 'The reason I gave you a piece of paper is because I love you and God loves you.' Since I had his attention, I thought I'd go ahead and invite him to church. So I said, 'And you need to come to my church and hear about this love I'm talking about.' "

One of the girls prompted, "And ... and ..."

"Well, the guy said, 'Ernie, if the people in your church are like you, it'd be a privilege to come to your church.' "

Some of the girls started crying. Ernie said, "I loved. I loved. Can we go on to another chapter?"

The kind of love Ernie showed can take us a long way in our Christian experiences. God's love is the one thing that makes us above average. We move beyond mediocrity toward excellence when we love others with God's love.

When we reach out our hand in love and someone goes *chop*, *chop*, we tend to bring it back. "See if I love you again," we say. Jesus calls us to stick out our hand again and again and again even if it gets chopped on. Because someday when we put out our hand, someone will say, "I want what you have."

If you want to know how to love more effectively, read 1 Corinthians 13. You will learn that love is patient, kind, protective, trusting, and persevering. Love never fails, and love never gives up. Paul wrote, "Now faith, hope, and love abide, these three; and the greatest of these is love" (1 Corinthians 13:13).

As you study 1 Corinthians 13, insert your name in strategic places. See how reading it as a personal letter makes it more powerful. For example, "If *Lori Salierno* has faith that can move mountains, but does not love, she is nothing." "If *Lori Salierno* is proud, envious, or rude, she does not have love." Anything that causes us to be less loving hinders our spiritual progress and blocks excellence out of our lives.

Daily Renewal

If you look at the distance you must travel as a Christian, you might be intimidated. You may not feel up to such a journey. That's okay. Presently, you don't have the resources within you to meet next year's spiritual challenges. That would be like expecting your body to run for the next year on today's food supply.

You won't receive a college diploma after completing one assignment, or even after completing the first semester's work. I could have blown my formal education if I had allowed one bad experience to get me down. I humbled myself and went back to that sociology class. I said, "Look, Salierno, perhaps you have an attitude problem. Get yourself in gear and start studying!" To make a long story short, I finished that degree and went on to earn a second degree simply by meeting the requirements one day at a time.

Daily renewal will also keep your spirit alive and vibrant. Paul understood this when he wrote, "Even though our outer nature is wasting away, our inner nature is being renewed day by day" (2 Corinthians 4:16).

If you want to go the distance with God, you must move ahead one step at a time. You can't sit around waiting for spiritual maturity to happen because it will not happen without effort on your part. You must progress day by day. As you absorb more of God's Word into your heart and mind, as you get to know God better through prayer, as you share God's love with others, you grow stronger for the journey.

It's okay to look ahead and decide where you want to be in your Christian life a year from now or ten years from now. You won't get there, though, unless you start moving in that direction. Each day you should ask yourself, "What can I do today to take me one step closer to my goal?"

Focus on Jesus

To accomplish a goal, you need focus. Focus determines how you will spend your time and money, what you think about, and where you direct your energy.

The stories about Jesus in the Bible provide focus for all who want to be long-distance Christians. "[Look to] Jesus the pioneer and perfecter of our faith.... Consider him who endured such hostility against himself from sinners, so that you may not grow weary or lose heart" (Hebrews 12:2–3).

When you fix your eyes on Jesus, how important is the latest fad? Is it really necessary to be part of the "in" crowd? Who cares if you make the team or even the honor roll as long as you have done your best? So what if your best friend turns against you? Does it matter if kids ridicule you for being a Christian? With your eyes fixed on Jesus, everything else pales in comparison.

You can sharpen your own focus by writing down everything in your life that is important to you. How many items on that list represent spiritual pursuits? Did you include Bible reading, church attendance, prayer, tithing, and witnessing for Jesus? If necessary, would you give up all that is on your list for Jesus?

If your focus does not center on Jesus as clearly as you think it should, you can reprogram your vision. Read in the Bible about how Jesus related to the world. Would anyone else die in your place? Where would you be without Jesus as your Redeemer? Considering the sacrifice he made for you, surely he deserves top priority in your life.

Did you know that a divine Jesus became human so that we might know God? "In [Christ] the whole fullness of deity dwells bodily" (Colossians 2:9). We don't get a partial reflection of God in Jesus; we get the full picture!

From the beginning Jesus was on the scene with God. Jesus took part in creation and participated in all the events in history. God planned for Jesus' role as Redeemer and Savior since before the world was created and promised it from Genesis through Malachi. Looking at that kind of record, you can be certain you can count on Jesus to help you endure to the end.

The Long Climb

I can't resist a challenge. When I found out I was going to Africa, I decided to climb Kilimanjaro. At 19,340 feet, Kilimanjaro is the highest summit in the world we can reach without supplemental oxygen.

Before I started the climb, I had some idea of what to expect. I knew it would take four days and a few unpleasant experiences before I reached my goal. Although I could not predict what difficulties I would face, I was prepared to overcome whatever obstacles I met.

As I placed one foot in front of the other, it seemed to make no difference in my progress toward the top. I kept thinking, I can hardly believe the way to conquer a mountain is by one step at a time.

I try to keep in shape by hiking, lifting weights, and biking. Even so, the four-day climb taxed my endurance. Did I ever think of quitting? Not on your life! Strained muscles and less-than-ideal overnight accommodations were a small price to pay for what I hoped to accomplish.

On the fourth day, our group started the climb at midnight. We wanted to reach the top as the sun came up. That last six-hour climb of nearly four thousand feet proved to be the hardest. Darkness made travel difficult. My feet were sore and my muscles ached, but I was so intent on reaching my goal I hardly noticed.

The view at the top of the mountain far surpassed what I imagined. Right before my eyes the snow changed colors to match the rising sun. Breathlessly, I took in the scene and somehow felt connected to heaven. Yet I knew I was experiencing only a fragmentary preview of the glory prepared for those who love God and endure to the end.

As much as I wanted to bask in thoughts of heaven, I forced my mind to return to earth. In my mind I saw masses of people. I saw unbelievers blinded by the god of this age. I saw struggling Christians. I wanted to join hands with Jesus and go forth to transform the world with him. I believe that same vision and energy can be yours for the long climb.

Will you go the distance with God? If you have ever felt like giving up, lift your eyes to heaven now and say, "God, I'll never quit on you!" Keep your love affair with God fresh through daily renewal. Focus on Jesus. When people fail you, when parents fail you, when teachers or friends disappoint you, fix your eyes on Jesus. Determine within yourself that no matter what happens, you're going to make it through. With Jesus on your side, you can do it!

God, I lift my heart in everlasting praise to you because you have redeemed me through the blood of Jesus. Thank you for your promise to take me through to the end. Help me feel your presence and know you are as close to me as my own breath. Draw me back to you if I should stray. In Jesus' holy name I pray. Amen.

***

How far do you hope to progress in your spiritual life during the next ten years?

_____

_____

_____

What portion of your goal do you expect to accomplish in the next year?

_____

_____

_____

What immediate step(s) will you take?

_____

_____

_____

"Now to him who is able to keep you from falling, and to make you stand without blemish in the presence of his glory with rejoicing, to the only God our Savior, through Jesus Christ our Lord, be glory, majesty, power, and authority, before all time and now and forever. Amen" (Jude 24–25).

Notes

Chapter 3

[1]Carl Sandburg, *Abraham Lincoln: The Prairie Years*, 2 volumes (New York: Harcourt Brace & Company, 1926).

Chapter 5

[2]Joni Eareckson, *A Step Further* (Grand Rapids: Zondervan, 1978).

Chapter 8

[3]*Reader's Digest Great Encyclopedic Dictionary* (Pleasantville, New York: Reader's Digest Association, 1975).

Chapter 12

[4]Booker T. Washington, *Up from Slavery* (Garden City, New York: Doubleday, 1963).

Chapter 13

[5]*Bartlett's Familiar Quotations,* "Address at Harrow School" (Boston: Little, Brown, and Company, 1980), 745.

For booking information for Lori Salierno, please contact:
Ambassador, Inc.
% Mr. Tim Grable
Post Office Box 50358
Nashville, Tennessee 37205

615–370–4700 (Phone)
615–661–4344 (Fax)